Learning

Use Accelerated Learning to Learn Any Subject or Language Quickly, Develop Laser-sharp Focus Instantly and Improve Your Memory

(Learning the Secrets of Speed Reading and Memorization)

Colin Mccullough

Published by Rob Miles

© **Colin Mccullough**

All Rights Reserved

Learning: Use Accelerated Learning to Learn Any Subject or Language Quickly, Develop Laser-sharp Focus Instantly and Improve Your Memory (Learning the Secrets of Speed Reading and Memorization)

ISBN 978-1-7771171-0-8

Legal & Disclaimer

The information contained in this book is not designed to replace or take the place of any form of medicine or professional medical advice. The information in this book has been provided for educational and entertainment purposes only.

The information contained in this book has been compiled from sources deemed reliable, and it is accurate to the best of the Author's knowledge; however, the Author cannot guarantee its accuracy and validity and cannot be held liable for any errors or omissions. Changes are periodically made to this book. You must consult your doctor or get professional medical advice before using any of the suggested remedies, techniques, or information in this book.

Table of Contents

Introduction

We live in an era of oversaturated markets and over communicated societies. It would be an understatement to say that our current world is continuing to become more and more competitive. In order to succeed in life and rise above the rest, one must be able to outperform everybody else. However, to get to the top, one must first need to possess the adequate capacity to make it there. With a limited scope of knowledge and experience, it is almost impossible to make it far. But the more evolved one's worldview and sophistication, the more one can apply their skills and wisdom to climb up the peak of life.

This is why education and constant learning are fundamental practices in success. There is not be a single successful person that is not continually pushing the barriers of his or her capabilities and increasing their mastery towards various fields. If you are to make an investment, invest not in material wealth or pleasure, but invest in yourself. Your single greatest asset is your mind, for everything in this world complies to worldly borders, but the mind knows no limits. You must think of your brain as a child; you must feed it, nurture it, and in turn it will grow and mature into the most magnificent wonder. Allow it to indulge in contentment, sloth, and gluttony however, and you will find it will perform no better than a cripple. Perpetually expanding the intellectual horizons of your brain not only provides you with more opportunities to thrive and excel, but also an understanding of everything beautiful in life.

Learning itself is not as simple as it sounds. As the world becomes increasingly more advanced and complex, the amount of things you need to learn well and learn fast continues to increase, while the time and resources available only seem to decrease. In order for you to successfully learn anything that's required for your personal success, you'll need to learn much better than most people. In other words, you'll need to learn how to learn. This is all in order to acquire the ability to assimilate new skills at a speed you have never experience before. It doesn't stop there though. To master anything, it requires you to continually practice upon it and sharpen those senses.

This is what this book is about. Within the pages of this book are several techniques that you can use to significantly improve the way you learn new things. And by doing so, you better your chances at striving for excellence and succeeding in life. Because knowledge is power, knowing how to learn just about anything well is the key to amassing such power necessary for triumph.

Let's begin.

Chapter 1: Attributes Of Accelerated Learning

Developing your mind to becoming a more efficient learner is an important aspect of thriving, surviving, and being a fulfilled human being in the world we live in today. The world is ever-changing, which makes it vital that we constantly seek out ways to remain present in relevant knowledge.

You are here because you wish you could learn things quicker and easier, right? The main aspect that sets accelerated learners from those just like yourself is the way they absorb the world around them each day. This chapter will bring to light the pertinent attributes that makes up an efficient, quick learner.

Being curious

Being an inquisitive individual is something that is powerful enough to fuel you to do anything you wish to do in life. The more curiosity you have within you, the more opportunities you will be presented to go further in life. Curiosity is indeed the fuel that can determine just how far you can go to your area of study. It is an aspect of learning that can be the difference between learning and learning at a rate in which you can soak in loads of information much faster. Being curious helps you to actually enjoy the process of becoming educated and mastering a skill. For those that are naturally curious, learning is an adventure. This causes them to seek out more information to answer their curiosity inquiries.

Humility

Those who are quick learners have respect for the weaknesses they possess. They are also very aware of the strengths they harbor too. Having knowledge about oneself will get you ahead in many ways. Those who are consciously aware of their strengths and weaknesses are better able to be independent learners. Meaning they are more than capable of setting grand priorities and can correct themselves when needed.

Process-oriented

Effective learners know the importance of enhancing the process of gaining a final product instead of the product. To be a good learner, you must have a process-oriented mindset. Focusing on the process should be far more important and intriguing than the result the process produces.

For example, when learning music, instead of concerning yourself about whether you can even play a piece of music, begin with focusing on honing the techniques that will allow you to play that piece successfully. Quick learners take the time to figure out what areas they are lacking and work on their problem areas.

There are quite a few benefits for those that live in the process-oriented mindset:

You have the patience to get through any process in its entirety. If you just focus on the result, you will never have the amount of patience necessary to go through the process of how you got to that result. When your focus in on the result, you may find yourself taking shortcuts that can lead to consequences in the end, or you simply give up on it altogether. Focusing on the process will provide you patience because you enable yourself to go through all the steps and see what the desired outcomes will be. Moreover, you get to enjoy the journey a heck of a lot more.

You can focus valuable energy on what is important. Being able to become a master of a certain skill takes a lot of energy. When you have a process-oriented mindset, you allow your mind to focus your energies on the important factors that help you to improve your techniques. You then do not waste precious energy worrying yourself over factors you cannot control.

Minimize your disappointment and levels of frustration. When focusing on just the product, you will more than likely end up disappointed when it does not turn out the way you wanted. However, when you consciously hone your mind in on the process to get to the result, you will not be overshadowed by such negative feelings. The goal is not to create what you need, but rather to improve yourself in every way possible.

Utilize what is learned

To successfully and completely learn something, you must learn to apply what you have learned and put it into action. Therefore, quick learners are advocates for participating in side projects. Projects of all shapes and sizes take time and energy, both of which are valuable. While you do not need to create a project for absolutely everything, learn to focus the projects you do get into on deepening your understanding on certain skill sets.

Successfully retain acquired knowledge

We are human beings. Everyone knows just how fast anything that is freshly learned can leave the human mind — almost as fast as the speed of light itself. This is why it is not only vital to learn new things properly, you must also learn how to retain it as well.

Taking notes is something many of us do, but quick learners typically do it more efficiently. They ensure that the notes they bother to take can trigger some sort of memory that will help them recall a certain set of information. When reading books, quick learners highlight important key points that express a broad point. This way, they are more than capable of reinstalling that knowledge later.

Synthetic thinking

Quick learners do not passively acquire knowledge. They do not just absorb information but are able to reconstitute what they learn into meaningful patterns that help them create mindful connections and insights. Quick learning is characterized by thinking and reading synthetically in a way that the context being soaked into the mind can grow, change and diverse itself.

Patience

For quick learners, having adequate levels of patience is directly correlated to a sustained effort with ultimate performance power. Having the kind of patience necessary to successfully be a fast acquirer of information takes time, dedication and lots of practice. Patience paired with persistence is essential to building a valuable, diverse foundation for creating reliable connections.

Relishing mistakes

Just like those who learn and retain information poorly, quick learners also make mistakes. It is the human way. The difference between poor and good learners is that good learners know how to grow from the mistakes they make. Mistakes, no matter the consequences, allow many opportunities to become readily available to us for the taking.

Quick learners lead a life with this mindset: "Success is never permanent, and failure is never fatal." This is why they are not frightened to take on challenges wherein they may not have the utmost confidence. They respect that there is constantly something to learn from brand new experiences, and this pushes them to venture into unfamiliar territory.

Diligently pursue understanding

Those that take pride in being a quick learner are dedicated to putting in the effort necessary to achieve a deep understanding of the knowledge at hand. They diligently seek out information to help them understand what they are trying to learn. They know that reading, analyzing and evaluating information are all vital steps to getting everything they can out of the information that is provided.

They know how to converse with other people about the subject, know where to find more reading materials and carry out processes that help them to understand parts of the information better. Until they thoroughly come to an understanding of it all. They think about it before sleeping, while working out, on their drive to work, etc. They also know when to listen intently to other individuals that may harbor the crucial information they have been looking for. Quick learners do not give up easily.

Recognize that not all learning is a blast

For quick learners, obtaining new and improved information is a journey that they like to take, but they know and embrace the fact that not all parts of the journey may be fun. However, this does not change their loving outlook towards learning new things and concepts. They get a thrill when all the pieces of the puzzle finally come together, and they can finally understand the concepts or skills they had been studying up on.

However, they know that some tasks on the path to understanding require the repetition of boring times, having mind-numbing attention to detail, and intense mental focus. They respect the body aches that come from sitting, the mess that their desks or working space may become, the stale taste of coffee. They know that these things mean they are on the brink of something great and trudge through them accordingly, not letting these aspects or other negative viewpoints get in their way.

Not immune to a fright

Good learners know that a part of successful learning is embracing the scared feelings that come along with the potential to fail. At the same time, they positively embrace the negative feelings, using them as motivation to dedicate themselves to the learning process. No matter how many times they fail, quick learners carry on, trying to figure out the information and crack the code within. They may become frustrated, but they use that as fuel towards their determination to find the knowledge they need to succeed and understand.

Create their own knowledge

This does not mean quick learners create their own version of the information they are trying to retain. It simply means they are all about making the new knowledge fit snuggly in whatever they already know. They know how to change their structures of knowledge so that they can accommodate what they are trying to absorb.

They utilize the new things they learn to tear down the information that is otherwise constructed poorly, finishing what was partially built and creating a new and improved structure. It is not only taking their own knowledge and running with it but also learning how to connect it to what they already are aware of in meaningful ways.

Always have questions

Quick and good learners know that they will never know everything about the world around them, which makes them realize that there is always more to learn. They are never quite satisfied with how much they are already knowledgeable of, and they let the curiosity within them drudge up more inquiries to acquire new and improved information continuously. They live alongside their questions and why they cannot adequately answer them. They are always seeking out new avenues that will hopefully lead them to an answer.

Share their knowledge

Knowledge, no matter how magical, is motionless unless it is passed on. If it is not shared, it is lost. Good learners are teachers in their own way, committed to sharing what they know with others. They write and have conversations about why they have learned. They are also capable of explaining what they know to others in various ways that help all sorts of individuals successfully soak in the information.

They understand that there are various ways to teach the information they know. They can paraphrase, translate, and create examples to help those understand the concepts they are trying to teach. They are masters at what they know and wish to teach and are committed to their knowledge being passed on to others in one form or another.

Think of themselves as lifelong students

Quick learners, no matter how seasoned in a subject, know that the amount of knowledge in the world far exceeds their lifetime to learn. Even for those that are teachers and coaches, they see themselves first as students themselves. This helps them to become less impressed with what they are knowledgeable of and more consciously aware of what they still need to learn and all the educational possibilities out there to explore.

Having pride versus being prideful

Successful individuals have plenty of pride and confidence, but good and quick learners are aware that having pride is much different from being prideful. Those that exhibit prideful ways do not take any sort of criticism well, constructive, or otherwise.

They can become quick to be defensive and are oversensitive about what other people are saying about them. They are not good at listening to the ideas of others and lack observational abilities. Too much pride or confidence is not a good thing; in fact, it can very well inhibit your ability to adequately learn, seek out needed advice, and admit your faults.

Self-critical

If you speak to anyone that is known to be a quick and efficient learner, they will tell you that they are their own worst critic. No matter what these people are told, more than likely they have already told themselves that criticism already. This helps them listen intently to the feedback of others without the feeling of defensiveness. For quick learners, input from outside factors helps speed up their learning processes and helps to improve their overall performance.

Sponge-like

When it comes to the concept of learning, many human beings live their lives as if they are a piece of silk, unwilling to absorb things around them. You will find that quick learners are much more like a sponge—extremely absorbent and can develop learning capabilities to harvest more information faster.

They tend to tune-in not only on key things but on broad spectrums that leave them hungry to hunt and find out more. This leads them to seek out experience and the insights from a variety of different individuals.

Seek the truth

Quick learners are constantly self-aware and are knowledgeable of themselves and what makes them tick. They are aware of and accept what they are both good and not so good at. They know what they have to offer to others and the world around them and embrace every piece of themselves, even the parts that may need a little work.

They also admit to themselves that there is plenty of information to still obtain and retain. This means they have set a grounded perspective for themselves that allows them to be exposed to a better variety of situations in a better and more appropriate fashion. They are humble, self-critical, and truly honest with themselves and so they are much better able to identify the areas they wish to pursue and which ones they need to work on improving.

Quick learners also understand situations that help them to build confidence in the abilities they possess. These aspects of their truth maximize their ability to learn at a faster rate and develop themselves more thoroughly to achieve their objectives in life and reach ultimate success.

Chapter 2: The Key To Accelerated Learning Of Languages

Learning a new language is difficult. The older you are, the more challenging it would be. Once the human brain is accustomed with the intricacies of one language, it tends to think in that language and hence learning a different and unrelated language becomes quite complicated. However, there are accelerated learning methods that you could use.

•Do not start with the dictionary or the grammar of the language. The grammar of a language is the most technical element. The dictionary or the entire vocabulary of any language will be vast and it would be incomprehensible, even for native speakers.

•Always start with the simplest method of all. Learn the most common words of a new language. You would notice that the most common words are used in greetings, expressions, responses or questions. Conversational language is the easiest to learn but you wouldn't succeed if you begin with the technicalities and from the ground up. It works when you are learning your native language or when a child is learning a foreign language. In such cases, there are no prevailing languages that one has already mastered and hence the brain is yet to start thinking in that language. The mind is more receptive and will remember the basics of the new language. Older people and those who have mastered one or more languages will not have this luxury.

•Once you learn the most common words, for example the fifty most commonly spoken words in Spanish or French, you should learn the most common sentences or phrases. Start with basics like 'hello' and 'how are you'. Proceed to 'I'm good' and 'thank you', then to the sentences that are most commonly used. You don't need to know the grammatical structure or nature of sentence construction just as yet. You can start to speak these common words and sentences. The mind will gradually get accustomed with these words and also remember their meaning.

•Words have no value without their explicit meaning. Learning a new language is difficult from both perspectives. Then there is the challenge of pronunciation. All these three challenges can be overcome with the aforementioned tips. Once you get accustomed with common words, sentences, the pronunciations and their meanings, you should proceed to learn new words. Over time you should start getting into the grammar.

The initial exercises shouldn't take you longer than a fortnight. They would set you on the path of accelerated learning of languages.

Chapter 3: Accelerated Learning

Accelerated learning is just that, it is an intense program that offers a student to learn a great amount of material in a much shorter amount of time. In society, as a whole, we have become very busy people. An accelerated learning program offers the opportunity for those students who may not be able to dedicate several years to a program, to go through that program and a far less amount of time. Therefore, making it much easier to fit classes into a busy schedule.

These types of programs can sometimes prove to be a bit of a challenge for students because, not a great amount of time is spent on each topic area. This could be an ideal situation for those who excel academically. One of the biggest benefits of an accelerated learning program, is that it gets students out of school and into the workforce quickly. This could be the ideal situation for parents who become students.

While the length of time is certainly a great perk to an accelerated learning program, it should be something that is carefully considered. If you find that you learn at a slower pace, or that you sometimes need more time spent on certain areas, you may find an accelerated program harder and maybe even a bit frustrating.

Generally accelerated classes work in terms rather than full semesters. A term can last anywhere from five to twelve weeks. Whereas, a semester lasts much longer. While you have a shorter amount of time to work with, often, more studying will be necessary to keep up with the pace of the class study. While the short time can be viewed as a perk, it can also mean less time for hands on approaches to the environment. This is certainly an option that may not necessarily fit each individual. While some may excel at the fast pace, others may find themselves struggling to take the information and keep up with the pace.

As with any educational choices, you have to research and make the decision that will work best for your situation. Should you decide that an accelerated learning environment is not for you, that is okay too. That is why it is known as merely an option. Whichever learning pace you decide is best for you and your situation, we do hope that you excel to your fullest potential and reach your goals in the process.

Chapter 4: Mental Prerequisites - Am I Suitable For Learning?

" The downside of intelligence is that one is constantly compelled to learn. "(George Bernard Shaw)

A) Objectives and expectations

For each new subject you want to learn, you should first ask yourself what expectations you have on the subject and what purpose they should lead to the working through the topic. This helps them to get an overview.

·Is it just to pass the exam in the subject somehow?

·Is she particularly interested in the subject?

·Is it a fundamental issue that should be given special attention because subsequent issues build on it?

·Is it an issue that they may have chosen themselves?

·Is there a practice reference to her other work?

Just thinking about the topic in the first place and asking questions about the objectives and expectations associated with the topic lead to a **subconscious analysis of the topic** before it reaches the detailed knowledge. It also helps to reveal and clarify the meaning and the scope of the topic, which can lead to a more intensive involvement in the topic and longer "on the ball".

B) Self-assessment / self-analysis - Can I do this?

Just as you question a new topic mentally, you should also question themselves. Have you already realized that the new topic is particularly complex or that they have no prior knowledge yet? Use these insights and connect them to **what they can do** .

·They go into an entirely new subject without prior knowledge, they plan more time for it than for a topic that they already know from the past in and out.

·Is it a topic with great technical and mathematical content and are not these areas so at all? Then they are already thinking about how to offset these deficits.

When they approach a subject in this way, they are subconsciously prepared for **possible** **difficulties** , can **prevent** and **plan** accordingly, frustration will spare them at best, because they are not caught cold. An honest self-assessment and analysis of one's own abilities related to the new topic are the cornerstones of successful learning planning.

C) Motivation - The tongues of the scale

" The best motivation is your own desire. "(Olaf Dohmen)

What is the purpose of your studies? What are your expectations? Study them because

·One expects it from them,

·Their supervisor wishes them,

·They want to accelerate their careers,

·It is financial or

·Social reasons

·Or do they need the degree as a formal requirement in the job or

·They have the desire to acquire high-quality knowledge in their field

·Is it their ambition that encourages them to complete their studies as best?

The quality of the energy that they put into the study and thus the learning of the individual contents, and thus the success of the entire study, is highly dependent on their motivation. They do not thereby underestimate the **role of their subconscious mind** . The more they burn, the more enthusiasm they show for studying, the easier it will be for them.

Intrinsic and extrinsic motivation - where does my motivation come from?

One differentiates two types of motivation, the **intrinsic** and the **extrinsic** motivation. Intrinsic motivation is when you do something **for your own sake** , simply because you have fun because it is satisfying, brings recognition, or simply doing good. Extrinsic motivation, on the other hand, is when you do **something** , **because you are promising an advantage** or avoiding a disadvantage.

Let us not imagine a self-study, as it is a distance study, is not easy to manage. In addition to the logistical, temporal and organizational aspects, it is particularly **difficult** to remain as constantly motivated as possible during the entire duration of the studies, not to buckle or even give up. **Intrinsic motivation has the greatest impact here** . The stronger your own will is something to be achieved, the less is the danger that we lose sight of the goal, thus the motivation. **In addition, extrinsic motivation can help us** . The more motivation we get from the outside, for example, through good examinations, recognition from colleagues, superiors and friends, the more we are ready to stay.

If motivation fails, or: How do you motivate yourself?

But what if the motivation is flattened, it may even give way to the frustration, the ambition fades and the self-doubt spread?

Then it is more than ever to prevent one from falling into lethargy and instead motivating itself. We must again mention the importance of the role of the subconscious. Draw the time after successful completion of studies. They will finally

·The desired promotion,

·to earn more money,

·Receive more recognition,

·They can finally take the professional path they dreamed of for so long.

·The evenings and weekends, where they have always had to learn, are now available for leisure, friends and family.

But the most important thing: **they have shown it to** themselves ! They have proved that they can do it, if they only want, if they only stay tuned. No one can take this **sublime feeling** of pride. Imagine now how it will feel if they have succeeded, despite all the adversities, despite the double burden of job and study. They have brought sacrifices in the form of leisure, weekends and spent energy. And now they are royally rewarded with a sense of pride. And rightly so!

TIP : Stay motivated. When they need to, they turn tricks at themselves to motivate themselves when things are not going so well.

Avoid excessive expectations by self-critically weighing the situation and setting realistic goals.

Chapter 5: Why Improve Your Learning Skills

Why is it so important to improve your learning skills? Let's discuss some of the reasons why you should make improving your learning skills a priority:

Sharp Learning Skills Help You Become Efficient, Productive, Alert, and Successful

Sharp memory and learning skills have a positive effect on every area of your life. Be it your personal or professional life, the benefits of these skills permeate every area of your life. If you learn things fast, you are likely to take less time to learn new things and information, be it related to your studies, your new office project, or your business.

Naturally, when you learn things fast, you take less time to go through any piece of information, which essentially means you have more time to do other things.

On top of that, good learning skills help you retain information quickly and recall any significant information in less time. When you remember information fast, this essentially makes it easier for you to take advantage of opportunities when they arise because as a fast reader and thinker, you can make informed decisions fast.

For instance, if your boss asks you and a few of your colleagues an important question about a current project and you answer it first, this is bound to leave quite an impression on your boss. In fact, because of this, your boss is likely to consider you for the position of team/project leader.

Moreover, excellent learning skills help you acquire new skills fast and master them quickly. Whether you are learning how to use Photoshop or how to play baseball, if you are sharp, focused, and alert, you are likely to acquire both skills fast and master them just as fast. Naturally, when you are skilled and efficient, you are likely to be productive, which increases your chances of achieving all your set goals and actualizing the success you want.

To cap this discussion, sharp cognition helps you learn, and do things fast, and pursue your goals and accomplish them. If you would like to learn things fast, skyrocket your productivity, and be the boss of your life, it is time you pay attention to your cognition.

The chapters that follow shall share amazing techniques that when implemented, promise to improve your cognition.

Chapter 6: How To Improve Your Memory And Learn Faster

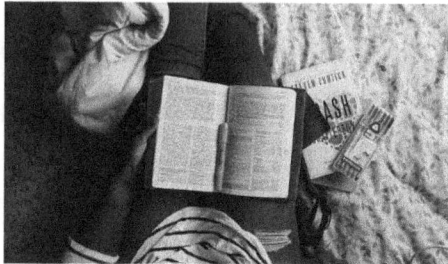

Learning fast is an important element if you want to be on top of your class or get a promotion at work. But learning will be useless if you can't recall the right information when you need it.

Experts in learning such as cognitive scientists and developmental psychologists have discovered a range of factors, which can help you to improve your memory and learn faster.

Advanced Strategies for Better Memory Recall

The following strategies could help you increase the chance of memory retention.

1. Pay Attention to the Material that you Are Learning

Attention is a crucial component of memory. To increase recall, information should be shifted from short-term memory to long-term memory. Your brain can do this if you focus your attention on the material that you are studying.

It is ideal if you have a designated space where you can study well. This place can be a corner in your room that is free from distractions such as street noise, TV, music, and other distractions.

Staying away from distractions could be difficult, especially if you have a roommate or you have small kids. You can schedule your study time and be sure that your roommate knows this special time so he would give you space. Meanwhile, you can ask your spouse to take care of the kids, so you can pay attention on your studying.

2. Avoid Multitasking

Watching TV, doing laundry, and studying at the same time will make it extra difficult for you to focus on any material that you need to learn. Even though it may seem that multitasking could help you to achieve more, research has shown that doing several things at the same time actually affects your accuracy and productivity. So if you want to learn more, be sure that you are not doing anything while you are studying.

3. Schedule Regular Study Sessions

Following a regular study schedule will prevent you from cramming. This will give you the time you need to process enough information. Research reveals that students who regularly study can remember the material far better compared to those who are studying the night before the exam.

4. Organize and Structure the Information that You Are Learning

Information is organized in related clusters. You can harness this structure by organizing the materials that you are learning. It is best to group similar concepts and terms together, or create an outline of your readings and notes to help you in grouping concepts.

5. Use mnemonics to improve memory recall

Mnemonics are effective tactics that you can use to help in better recall. Basically, a mnemonic is a special method of remembering information. For instance, you could associate a particular group of concepts, which you can remember with a more common term that you can easily remember. Ideally, mnemonics should be used with novelty, humor, and appealing imagery. You could come up with a song, a rhyme, or a joke, which could help in recalling a certain information.

You can use name mnemonics or expression mnemonics. A good example of a name mnemonic is PVT. TIM HALL for remembering the names of essential amino acids: Phenylanine, Valine, Threonine, Tryptophan, Isolucine, Histidine, Arginine, Leucine, and Lysine.

Below are the examples of expression mnemonics:

To easily remember Henry's Law: Pressure can increase gas solubility, you can use this expression - To remind you of good ol'

Henry, take note of the bubbles in the shaken Cola you drank.

To easily remember Boyle's Law: Pressure is inversely proportional to volume at constant temperature, you can use this expression – Boyle's law is best of all, because it presses gas really small.

6. Practice Makes Perfect

To better retrieve information, you need to ingrain what you are learning into long-term memory. For example, if you need to learn key terms in chemistry, you can study these terms and then read a more detailed description on the meaning of that term. After practicing this process several times, you will notice that information retrieval is a lot easier.

Meanwhile, experiencing the actual application of the concept can help you in better recall. Hence, reading chemical equations is not enough. You need to actually test out the theories in the lab.

Connect New Concepts to Things That You are Familiar With

Once you are learning a material that is unfamiliar to you, you can take the time to think how about this new concept is related to the things that you already know. By linking new ideas to your existing memories, you can significantly increase the chance of recalling information that you have recently learned.

For example, if you are learning calculus, think of ways that you can apply the theories in more common things such as how you can use the concepts in daily life such as electricity, magnetism, etc.

Visualize Ideas to Enhance Memory and Recall

You can enhance your memory and recall if you try to visualize the information that you are studying. Probably you have noticed that it is easier to study a textbook filled with graphics, charts, and pictures. If you don't have any visual cue to help, you can create your own. You can draw figures or charts alongside your notes or you can use different colors of pens or highlighters to cluster related ideas in your study materials.

Teach New Information to Your Colleague

Research reveals that reading out loud considerably enhances the memory recall. Learning specialists also discovered that the actual teaching of new information to other people improves understanding and information retrieval. You can use this strategy in your own studies by teaching the information that you have learned to a class mate, a roommate, or a study buddy.

Double Your Efforts to Focus on Difficult Learning Material

Have you realized that it is easier to recall information found in the first and final chapters? Research reveals that the sequence that the information is presented could play a role in recall. This is known as the serial position effect.

Even though retrieving information found in the middle of a textbook could be difficult, you can resolve this problem by taking extra time in practicing the concepts. You can also try restructuring what you have just learned, so it could be easier to recall. If you stumble upon a really difficult concept, you can exert extra effort to really learn and understand the new information.

Change Your Study Habit Once In a While

Another effective strategy to enhance your memory is to change your study habits once in a while. If you have been studying inside your room for three days in a row, try to move to another place for your next study schedule. If you are studying at night, you can spend several minutes every morning to review the concepts that you have studied. Be more creative on how you study. With this, you can enhance the effectiveness of your efforts and considerably enhance your long-term memory.

Get Enough Sleep

Another area, which researchers are now exploring is the effect that sleep deprivation has on the learning process. Without enough sleep, you tend to become less alert, attentive and focused, which make it extra difficult to absorb knowledge. Sleep deprivation results in over-worked neurons, which can no longer work properly to properly link information, and we lose our capacity to recall previously learned knowledge.

Also, our processing of interpretation could be affected. Our capacity to make sound decisions are affected as our mind is not properly well suited to assess the situation and react accordingly. Our judgment can be affected.

Over fatigue could affect our ability to learn. Our organ systems doesn't work at optimum, muscles are not relaxed, and neurons don't fire rapidly. Lapses in concentration as a result of sleep deprivation could even result to physical injury and accidents, which is crucial if you are training hands-on such as sports and machine functions.

Not enough sleep also has negative effects on individual moods, which also affect learning. Mood alterations affect our capacity to absorb new information and consequently recall that knowledge. Even though persistent sleep deprivation affects different people in different ways (and the effects are not completely explored), it is already a fact that high quality sleep has a positive effect on learning and memory.

The NASA Nap

Taking a nap seems to be a habit for slackers, but research suggests that it can help you in maximizing your learning ability, whether you are mastering rocket propulsion or you just learning how to knit.

In 1995, NASA has conducted a special research among their pilots to help them become more alert, which is crucial for their job. The result of the research suggests that a 26-minute nap in flight (while the NASA pilots are still at work) increased their performance by 34% and general alertness by 54%.

Taking the NASA nap can help you learn more as it serves as a quick fix to rest your body and mind. The ideal time to take a NASA nap is between 1 pm to 4 pm, and you should also lay down with your head and upper body elevated (like a sitting position) to avoid REM and deep sleep.

If you are working on a large learning project, it is recommended to take a mid-day snooze or a restorative nap. Set your clock timer for 26 minutes. If you want a longer nap, set it for 90 minutes, so you can complete a whole sleep cycle and wake up feeling rested and ready to learn again.

Exercises

Go over the strategies discussed in this chapter. Choose the best tips that you can use based on the nature of the material that you need to study. Be sure to practice these strategies regularly.

Chapter 7: Preparing Your Body

One of the most important things you can do to help you become a memorization wiz is to take care of yourself. By ensuring that your system is running at its best you will give your mind the best shot possible to retain information. A body that is sleep deprived or not given the proper fuel will not function as well as one that is. So by following a few of these simple steps you will set your mind up for success and making learning and retaining what you have learned that much easier.

Get enough sleep, it cannot be stressed enough how important sleep is. Try to get at least 7 hours of sleep a day, a well rested mind is more prepared to retain information and is just more ready to work in general. Also minimize your blue light exposure before going to sleep, so avoid computers, your phones, and TV before bed.

Try to keep yourself well hydrated. If you can keep water or maybe even some unsweetened tea, sugar will defeat the exercise, your body and brain will be able to better function getting the water that it needs to live off of.

Sugar can be your enemy in the case of studying, it may seem like a great jolt to keep you going but the crash can stop you in your tracks and make things worse for you. The excess energy can be the wrong kind making your more fidgety then able to sit and focus like you may need to.

Walk or exercise on a regular basis if you can. The better your body function the healthier you will feel and your brain will feel. You are also more likely to feel happier and better about yourself and this lift in mood can make focusing and studying that much easier.

Try to avoid stressors and schedule out your day to a certain degree so you can reach optimal productivity during your day. Not only will you feel like you have accomplished something it will help keep you from stressing about things you need to accomplish because you will already be preparing your brain.

Chapter 8: Create The Right Learning Environment

Just about every task you can think of has a proper place where it should be performed. For example, cooking should take place in a kitchen, car repairs should take place in a garage, and exercise should take place in a gym. You probably wouldn't make the mistake of trying to cook dinner in the garage, and you probably wouldn't expect to get your daily workout done in the kitchen. That said, far too many people expect to be able to learn a topic effectively in just about any environment imaginable. You have probably seen people studying in libraries, and that makes sense. However, you have also probably seen people studying in buses, on the train, outside, and in their bedroom. This is often where so many people fall short when trying to learn any subject, no matter how large or small it may be. Just as it is critical to find the right location to do a workout, cook a meal or fix a car, so too is it critical to find the right environment for studying.

The right environment for studying can be a tricky thing to find. All too often people assume that a quiet, distraction free environment such as a library is the only place where a person should study. The truth of the matter is that every person reacts to environments in different and unique ways. For some people the silence and solitude found in a library can be the perfect environment for studying and learning a new subject. However, for others the same silence and solitude can actually be detrimental. Therefore, the trick to learning any new subject matter isn't about finding the right place to study, rather it is about finding the place to study that is right for you. Subsequently, the very first thing you will want to do is to experiment with different locations in order to find the one that feels right and that provides the best results.

Needless to say, distractions can be the biggest enemy to anyone who is trying to study. Whether the distractions are sounds, such as the TV or a radio, or whether they are objects to interact with, or even other people, anything that distracts you from being able to concentrate is a huge problem. Therefore, the number one thing that you need to do is to figure out what elements act as distractions for you. Try studying in a quiet environment for an hour and see how well you are able to stay focused while reading the material at hand. Then try to study for an hour listening to music and see how well you can stay focused under those conditions. One way will prove more beneficial than the other as some people need silence in order to focus, whereas others require noise in order to drown out the chatter that can plague your mind. Once you figure out whether or not you need silence then you will be able to choose a study location more effectively.

Another variable that will affect your ability to concentrate is the amount of activity going on around you. Like sound, some people require ambient activity in order to concentrate, whereas others become too distracted if anything is going on around them. The important thing is to discover which conditions help you to stay focused on the information you are trying to learn. Therefore, try studying for an hour in a place where no one is around, such as your bedroom or some other private location. Next try to study for an hour in a place where people are coming and going, such as a park, a coffee shop or some other relatively peaceful location that has ambient activity going on. This activity can be soothing or it can be distracting, depending on your personality. Determining which works best for you is critical for being able to get the most from your study time.

Once you have experimented with different locations the next thing to consider is the time of day that is best for your studies. Some people are able to learn more when they study first thing in the morning, while others are better suited for afternoon study sessions, or even late night learning. Again, your personality will determine which conditions are good for you and which ones are bad. The all important thing is that you find the time that works best for you as this will help you to maximize the results of your efforts. Using the same technique for trying to study for one hour at the different times is the best way to finding the ideal time slot for you.

Once you have determined the ideal location, environmental conditions and time of day to study the next step is to put all of these variables together in order to discover your ideal learning environment. You may find that late night library sessions are perfect for you, or you may discover that early morning study sessions in a coffee shop are the way to go. Don't worry about whether or not it makes sense, just focus on doing what works best for you. That is the first step in developing successful learning habits that will enable you to learn any subject quickly and effectively.

Chapter 9: Strategies To Expand The Mind'spotential

As we have discussed throughout this book, learning is a whole body exercise, but that does not lessen the importance of the brain in the whole process. There are many students who feel limited by such things as their own IQ, or what they deem to be mental deficiencies. How can a teacher assist their student to overcome these perceived negatives to create a positive learning environment?

One of the best methods for doing so is by using environmental tools, such as music. There are researchers that have created at least four different strategies with music alone. Throughout this chapter, we will explore these four strategies and how to incorporate them into our learning techniques. The results can encourage a student and help them to create a positive learning environment to build their knowledge base.

Simply put, music can be used to enhance mood and memory. Thus, it can have an effect on how much a student absorbs, but also how much they are able to retain throughout the learning process. When listening to certain music, IQ and learning capability are enhanced, at least when the music is playing in the background. So what are the best musical pieces to use for mental enhancements? Classical pieces, including Mozart, Bach and Beethoven, have all demonstrated the ability to increase IQ as well as building an individual student's learning speed.

The University of California at Irvine has been the home of research on the effects of music on learning. The researchers found that those who listened to Mozart had an increase in their spatial IQ test by roughly nine points, while those who listened to a relaxation tape saw only a one point increase. Those subjects that did not listen to any music scored the lowest on the test. Researchers found that music did have a positive effect, but they also saw the effects did not last long after music ended. Still, by keeping this music as part of a student's learning process, a student can enhance their mental abilities with regular and more permanent long term results.

So how can one add music to their life on a regular basis? A student can do so by means of musical lessons. When musical lessons are part of a student's learning environment, they can often find themselves putting puzzles together faster than those who did not have musical lessons in their lives. Other research has shown that the benefits of music can best be captured with tasks that require the individual to create or engage in a task with mental imagery. When a task did not use mental imagery, the researchers found that music or even music lessons had little to no effect on the individual's ability to complete the task.

For young children, music lessons can provide benefits that last a lifetime. Their abilities when it comes to mental imagery can be extensive. Additionally, music has a relaxing effect on the brain, making it easier for a student to move into an active learning capacity. This ties into other research that found specific music and verbal inflections can be combined to create a natural and rhythmic memory aid as we shall see.

Out of that research came the Active and Passive Concerts. The Active Concert is best used with material that needs to be read. It combines verbal methods with relaxation and music. When building the Active Concert, one must read the information out loud in time with the music. Adding emotional flair helps to engrain the information even deeper into the brain of the student. The musical highs and lows provide a unique tempo for the reading. Additionally, the student is engaging their whole body by adding the rhythm to the reading. Then the ears and mouth get into the picture by both hearing and reading at the same time. Thus, the student is engaging with all of their senses. As we have learned, this promotes long term retention. Thus, music has a positive effect all the way around for a student.

Passive Concerts also follow the same tactics, but they use a softer voice and different musical backgrounds to create the effect. Researchers have found that these concert methods have long term effects on the memory and retention of new information. Beethoven is one composer that was found best for the Active Concerts, while Bach worked better with the Passive Concerts. Still, it is easy to see how engaging the brain on multiple levels using music can have some pretty amazing results for students.

Researchers have found that engaging with multiple senses, essentially information that we hear, see, say and do can result in a ninety percent retention rate. The percentages go down significantly if only one sense is involved in the learning process. Therefore, it is important to find ways to add multiple senses to any learning experience. Reading a chapter of a textbook for a particular class? Try reading the text out loud to music. By matching the words to the rhythm, one can create a memory aid while engaging at least two or more senses. Long term retention has been demonstrated to increase time and time again because one is able to engage with the information in a multilevel fashion.

Mental imagery is another method that researchers have found to be conducive to accelerated learning. As we learned in the early part of this chapter, music was affective in helping individuals learn mental imagery tasks, such as puzzles. But the use of mental imagery can be taken away from music and used on its own. Our imaginations provide us the ability to create pictures and imagery simply by reading the words on a page. Old time radio shows were designed to engage with their listeners' imaginations. Thus, the listeners provided the imagery themselves. There are some who believe that movies and television have reduced our brain's ability to create their own mental imagery or mental pictures. No matter where you fall on that argument, it is important to understand that mental imagery aids learning. So reading out loud, or pausing in your reading to build a mental scene, can help your imagination to flex its muscles. This will build your mental capabilities over the long haul and assist in your ability to retain larger chunks of information as part of the creation of a student's knowledge base.

Two specific memory options are also available to a student. One is to create a metaphor or an exaggerated story to match information one is trying to retain. For example, one can build a story around a list, using the words in the list as standouts within the story. Your brain can thus create a mental picture that will help you to remember the list in a long term fashion. When paired with an association technique, such as pairing the exaggerated story to music, a student can quickly find that they will remember the information within the story for a significantly long period of time.

After reading through the story along with the music, one should easily be able to recall the necessary information. But the important thing to remember that the story needs to have some pretty extensive exaggerations. After all, if the brain cannot build a wild mental image, this memory key will not be nearly as effective. However, it can be used with lists, chunks of information and even strategic plans.

Yet none of this is worthwhile if your student does not have a positive attitude toward the learning process. These techniques are not going to be as effective if they met with a negative attitude or scepticism. If your student is struggling, then it is important to encourage them by asking such questions as what do they gain from acquiring the information? A teacher can sometimes reach their student by simply appealing to their greed. After all, we all tend to work harder when we believe we will be benefiting in some way. Learning a new skill, for example, might result in a raise at our student's place of employment. But if they cannot learn the skill with a long term retention, it will do them little good. So you must help them to find that positive attitude. This goes back to the point of creating a positive and welcoming learning environment. So what is another method that students can use to reach that positive point of view? For many students, reflecting on periods of intense joy or success can bring them to a positive frame of mind. But how does one rebuild or recapture a feeling associated with an experience that happened years or even decades ago?

In the next chapter, we will discuss how the use of guided meditation can be effective in both memory enhancement, but also in creating a positive mental state for your students to flourish within. By following the method of guided meditation outlined, one can reach back into your past for some of the best feelings of your life and bring them forward to your learning experience in the present.

Chapter 10: Strategies To Help Develop A Photographic Memory

A photographic memory, or eidetic memory as it is now and again called, is the capacity to see a picture, a scene, or a page just once and later reviewing everything about what was seen without taking a gander at it once more. It is anything but the expertise that everyone has, and the majority of the general population who have this specific capacity are brought into the world with it. Nonetheless, it is conceivable to prepare the cerebrum and upgrade memory aptitudes in any person from the all-inclusive community until they have the practically immaculate review that the vast majority brought into the world with eidetic capacity have.

A great many people feel that eidetic and photographic memory are the equivalent, which isn't generally valid. The eidetic mind is the capacity to see a picture and later review even the smallest subtleties of that picture. This can happen even without appreciating what that picture truly is. A photographic memory is the capacity to consider that similar picture with an ideal understanding of what the subtleties are and what they mean. Notwithstanding, if it is conceivable to build up a photographic memory to the degree of having the option to have eidetic capacity is as yet not indisputably demonstrated.

There are numerous manners by which individuals have attempted to build up their very own recollections to such boundaries, as having such a close flawless memory can be useful to anyone.

Various Strokes for Different Folks

School trains youngsters by methods for having them continue everything, at that point by partner what they realize with different ideas. They are educated in approaches to enable them to recollect data all the more effectively. For example, to recall what certain expressions or words mean, they are trained to utilize them in sentences and short stories. You can say they build up a photographic memory of those words by affiliation.

Many individuals experience difficulty reviewing numbers and sets of numbers. They are probably the hardest things to recollect. Individuals who have figured out how to create photographic recollections probably won't need to connect names with pictures; however, have a kind of capacity bank inside their cerebrums where they document data identified with numbers.

More than one examination has demonstrated that eidetic memory, not to be mistaken for photographic memory, is unprovable. Anyway, there are speculations which express that youngsters may have some eidetic memory which is lost as they become more seasoned. It is conceivable to prepare the cerebrum to a limited degree, potentially even to build up a photographic memory. The strategies used to make can be changed and extraordinary. The fact of the matter is if your favored technique is completed long enough, you will encounter a lift in memory control.

Double the Reading Speed and Astonish Others

People some of the time get disappointed because they fall behind when perusing and learning because of the enormous measures of reading material they should assimilate for school or work. Such vast numbers of books are being composed around the world, that perusers in some cases experience issues staying aware of the generation of fiction and true to life works. It tends to be genuinely stunning, attempting to stay informed of everything " don't you think.

In the expediently changing and exceedingly focused business world, with new items and administrations, and new redesigns presented each week, speed perusing indeed proves to be useful. Most corporate moguls presently examined a few business-related books each week. That is a great deal of work for those unfortunates who don't have speed perusing capacities.

Speed Reading empowers people adolescent ought to be taken in up to multiple times or 3 x whatever they generally contemplate inside once.

Perusing analysts recently decided the intellectual capacities are fit for understanding and inventorying through ten,500 to 60,000 models of information each minute. Along the unit is a roughly single word. The body's five sentiments are receptors for subtleties, which as a rule this gets in the specific profundities of the mind-brain to be recorded concerning posterity. When the mindful musings need nuances, it is have been in the oblivious. Next, it surfaces the necessary information concerning running and utilizes, like your PC.

A decent correspondence is accessible in the middle of the mind, that correctly think about how the PC Computer, and the cerebrum that comprises of emotions and furthermore contemplations. Practically all data will get handled such that we may find it.

The data that people acquire, procedure, and furthermore evaluate begins from our five physical, substantial resources. Alongside which information, our cerebrum can settle on decisions, decisions, and judgment making. We all find utilizing our own five sentiments (i.at the. locate, smell, perusing, feel, taste), which are already pre-modified to react in a flash.

A genuine case of pre-modified activity: Consider the case of the high schooler kid who scents pizza and what his response is. It is like Pavlov's canine since his faculties make an impression on the mind as an idea.

The impression of inclination our preferred sustenance is a mental exercise, contrasted with the response of gulping, which is physical. In this manner, cerebrum and the brain is the place the activity is, and the body is the place the answer is.

Contemplating this strategy concerning speed considering can inspire the utilization of 3 from the five detects. That is a technique that will firmly impact proper exertion into the recall, recollect and fathom; well beyond in which, properly train you Means of being much better and increasingly effective per users.

Do as trained, and you'll transform into any speed per users that want to inspect as improve the gauge of his or her very own living. We accept incredible, decisive triumphs of your stuff with fabulous progressions in a few places you will ever have.

Information: The regular United states secondary schoolmaster (I comprehend this appears to be odd, yet some are graduating without to have the option to learn at an extraordinary eighth quality stage), filters from around 200 terms every single moment. A fantastic understudy peruses 20% quicker with 300 words every single moment. Notwithstanding precisely what your standard or maybe starting examining rate will be, your very own planned scanning speed in the wake of utilizing these sorts of systems will be all the more rapidly in addition to your potential is exceptionally boundless. It is because scientists who have investigated the human cerebrum/mind assent our conceivable is endless. Twofold triple-fourfold your perusing speed, there is just no limitation.

You can hope to figure out how to accomplish your most unique possibilities as a per user, specialist, understudy, and so on. This is because you're turning into a constant speed per user and a total accomplishment throughout everyday life.

Be Dynamic Through Speed Reading will enable you to turn out to be boundless in your capacity and capacity to do, be, and have all that you need throughout everyday life, regardless of whether its incredible evaluations or budgetary achievement.

Step by step instructions to Read Better and Faster

Most understudies and experts might want to figure out how to peruse better and quicker to ace more significant volumes of data and invest more energy doing the things they appreciate. When you've never done any examination on the best way to improve your perusing aptitudes, you may accept that it is impossible you can peruse better and quicker because our perusing rates are fixed. If this were valid, at that point everybody would read at a similar speed.

In any case, there is consistently somebody who can peruse preferable and quicker over you, and this is because they have accepted the time and open the door to learn speed examining systems and actualize them in their lives.

Figuring out how to peruse better and quicker through speed, perusing has various points of interest. Above all else, you get the chance to read more sections in far less time, which extends your database and makes you educated about various things. Besides that, you likewise get a more excellent vocabulary, expanded fixation, better relational abilities, and improved fixation and core interest. The best part about figuring out how to peruse better and quicker is that it doesn't take four years of diligent work to get familiar with the procedures to speed perusing. You should put aside, at any rate, ten minutes consistently to rehearse these essential systems, and you will peruse better and quicker in the blink of an eye.

The secret to figuring out how to peruse better and quicker is to maintain a strategic distance from the negative behavior patterns that hinder our scanning speed. One of these is called sub-vocalization - the propensity for perusing the words so anyone can hear as you read them. Attempt to act naturally mindful when you read, and catch yourself when you discover your lips moving alongside the content. By taking out this propensity, you'll realize how to peruse better and quicker in the blink of an eye. Another of these negative behavior patterns is back-skipping or glancing back at words and sentences you've just scrutinized. Back-skipping, as a rule, happens when the peruser is staring off into space or is just half-centered around the content in front. To keep yourself from back-skipping, ensure you're perusing in a reasonable, agreeable condition free from undesirable diversions. By reading in a spot that is helpful for learning, you'll see that you can understand better and quicker as a result of the expanded concentration and focus.

When you practice how to peruse better and quicker, ensure you work on utilizing a content that is anything but difficult to read. Try not to attempt to improve your speed reading abilities using a confounded specialized manual with bunches of language! The best perusing material to rehearse on is a paper or magazine article on a theme you find fascinating. Like this, you'll have some good times figuring out how to peruse better and quicker, and you'll discover some new information about a point that interests you as well.

You can likewise buy a speed perusing program in case you're not kidding about figuring out how to read better and quicker. Speed perusing projects contain every one of the mysteries and traps to improving as a per user, and the more significant part of them have unconditional promises if you don't want twofold you're perusing speed. So if showing yourself how to read better and quicker isn't working, consider giving the experts a chance to enable you to out.

Why We Need to Learn Accelerated Learning Techniques

A few teachers would state that the center of quickened learning system is disguising the date with the utilization of the components of life. There is no utilization of power or control to defeat the method. Ordinarily, educators would consolidate life's elements, and they would now be able to bring the most out of the information without getting exhausted by any means. Each understudy is getting a lot of information while learning in an entirely agreeable condition.

In any circumstance, an agreeable physical condition assumes a significant job in learning, particularly when you're applying the procedures of quickened learning. It equips each effort towards making a happy with learning condition for the understudies. The correct temperature, lighting, plants, shade of the divider, the furniture utilizes, and even the design has a significant influence in giving the best happy with learning condition for the understudies.

Different reasons why we have to become familiar with this procedure is because it tells us techniques on the best way to fortify the exercises. A guide to this is the utilization of visual guides or any peripherals that will help animate the intuitive personality while the understudy concentrates his or her eyes on the educator. Visuals help in getting understudies consideration and in this manner, at last, help them adapt rapidly.

Another motivation behind why we have to gain proficiency with this procedure is for us, instructors, to have the option to give the most out of the data and have the opportunity to convey it to the understudies without exhausting them. Instructors are capable of each tyke's learning. When we don't ace this method, we probably won't almost certainly show the children fabulous. The quickened learning procedure encourages us like the correct utilization of our tone. Without the educators' direction, the understudy may think that its difficult to learn and review immense measure of information.

Additionally, another reason is that it's a quick-paced world out there; everybody should be focused to exceed expectations at what they're doing. This can be at school or work. It's concentrate at work as well. You must be speedy at engrossing all data, or else you'll get a reminder and possibly get terminated.

The procedures can help us in any field that we are in. It tends to be utilized at school as well as in our calling. We as a whole need to be focused, and we need to stay aware of what's is happening now. We can beat and embrace current changes in case we're devoted to figuring out how to receive to change and be focused by learning rapidly.

The Benefits of Accelerated Learning Techniques

Quickened learning strategies handle the association between your body and your psyche and will utilize the data from the eyes, ears, and contact to learn. Given by the instructor's comprehension and supervision will help the cerebrum work and license it to develop innovative and imaginative addresses. The answer for effective routine with regards to quickened learning strategies is keeping up the dauntlessness between customary address and non-traditional addresses.

A case of these learning systems incorporates using music to impact the passionate condition and the state of mind of each student. The impact of music can be colossally profitable for an instructor wishing to bond with students on a blend of subjects.

The thoughts of quickened learning likewise comprise of the first convictions of non-cognizant education. The utilization of music in educating is a methodology that licenses for this system to occur. If you blended the music while learning loads of students will have a great time and when they have a fabulous time, their psyches would be viable simultaneously, and they can think about a variety of things. That is, as of now demonstrating the viability of learning.

Quickened learning systems can exceptionally affect students whose exhibitions are truly low that varies over a wide range. This is for those students who get uninterested and lose fixation in a subject.

As a run of the mill of training, educators should continue boosting their final product of advances in capability and mind look into. It is dependent upon them to assemble critical elements of such data to their students to make their investigations alive and educated. It is dependent upon them to impart in their students' brains the significance of this data for their future. These methods are useful to develop the psyches of the youthful students to have the option to accelerate their learning and have the opportunity to get in with the world's requests.

Quickened Learning Techniques - Tips and Tricks

So you need to learn quickened learning? Perhaps you have known about it from companions, or possibly you thought that it was on the web, or hell maybe you know the vast majority of the methods and aptitudes.

This chapter is heard about attempting to support you.

So here we go! Ahead to our quickened learning methods!

1. Mental aides. Memory aids are one of the top approaches to retain anything rapidly. Become accustomed to making a relationship to recall things.

2. Utilize your faculties Want to recall the atomic structure of a particle? Need assistance remembering essential (or troublesome) words for English? This is, perhaps the ideal ways! While considering it partner it with at any rate three detects, so close your eyes and see the word, recipe, or whatever structure in your brain. Make it move around when it enters as well and include a sound. To finish it off include a smell or perhaps a splendid shading. Or on the other hand, you could do both. This system is unquestionably the best.

3. Use mind mapping I could complete an entire book on this system! What you need to do is take Associations and memory aides to the additional level. Each time you hear, see or think something partner it with something simple to recall. At that point at whatever point you have to review something utilize the law of Association. This works superior to anything it sounds, trust me on this. I used to question it as well.

4. Focus! This is quickened learning? Here is a little thing I adapted some time in the past, to get any strategy to work you have to focus on what you are learning, all the more regularly than not our cerebrums our half sleeping. To fix this issue give denoting a slice a shot your paper each time you space out, this won't just bring you back, however, help you understand what you have to chip away at.

The Secret Habits of Highly Productive People

So how would you become highly productive?

To start with, you should guarantee that your objectives and targets are recorded as a hard copy. For every purpose and goal, it is additionally essential to list what you're attempting to achieve, alongside your inspiration driving why completing those objectives and destinations matter.

When this is finished, the subsequent stage is to make a point by point activity plan(s) for accomplishing those objectives and goals. Make sure to feature, and organize, every one of the means required, alongside including activity owner(s) and courses of events. By organizing your objectives and destinations, you'll realize where to center your time and vitality, consequently being progressively proficient, viable, and productive.

If it's not too much trouble guarantee that you comply with the time constraints that were presented, particularly for significant objectives and goals, the aim isn't to list unrealistic courses of events for accomplishing your objectives however to take into account satisfactory time to achieve every one of the undertakings recorded with the quality that it merits.

Last, and above all, is the focus. To be highly productive and useful, you should be able to focus your gifts and capacities on finishing assignments with the most noteworthy yield. Keep in mind, one of the fundamental objectives is to distribute your gifts and abilities so that you accomplish the most noteworthy conceivable profit for the vitality you put into any undertaking or task. To guarantee that your time and energy is apportioned carefully, it's ideal for concentrating and focussing on errands that take into account your qualities. The reason being is that you do things that you're great at, not exclusively will you be increasingly productive while having a fabulous time yet also commit fewer errors all the while, in this way submitting higher nature of work.

What's more, you should likewise guarantee that you center around the chances of things to come instead of tending to the issues of the past. This idea is like how fruitful associations utilize their assets - the gifts of their best individuals are distributed to the best up and coming open doors for the firm. As opposed to concentrating your vitality on a ton of unremarkable undertakings that includes no genuine worth, individuals must utilize their assets to focus on assignments that have any effect. By concentrating your endeavors on crucial territories, you'll have the option to accomplish the most critical outcomes at all measure of time.

If it's not too much trouble, note that highly productive individuals don't race through their errands. Instead, these people keep up an enduring work pace mood that enables them to finish a colossal measure of work without getting to be restless or pushed. The reason being is that highly productive individuals have figured out how to ace the craft of "center and fixation" for significant errands that will have a positive effect in accomplishing their objectives and goals throughout everyday life and they don't stop until their assignment is finished!!

Step by step instructions to Make Money and Become More Productive

A great many people would prefer only not to profit; they need to get more cash-flow. Sadly the more significant part believes that they will achieve this by working harder and more. They neglect to understand that the way to making more cash is in ending up increasingly productive. Thus the need is to work more efficiently. Here are a couple of tips that I have learned as an entrepreneur that has helped me to become increasingly productive.

Worth your time. It has been said that "time is our most valuable ware," and separated from great wellbeing I would state that this announcement is valid. We, as a whole, know the inclination when somebody demonstrates an absence of thankfulness for our time. Regularly individuals who treat others with this absence of respect don't esteem their own time either. To become progressively productive, don't waste your most valuable item and set clear limits with the goal that others will appreciate your time as much as you do.

Be great at what you do. There are the individuals who will work as long as they can remember squeezing out a living basically because they are average at what they do. Specialists are well known for this. Abstain from becoming hopelessly enamored with a lifelong way before surveying if you incline the work. Being straightforward with yourself in such a manner will pay profits. Find what you are excellent from the start, at that point figure out how to appreciate doing that.

Have an activity. One of my preferred proverbs states: "He that is watching wind won't plant." If you are trusting that the ideal minute will venture out accomplishing something, that minute is never going to come.

Be focussed and organize assignments. There is another platitude that, "if one doesn't know where they are cruising, no wind is a decent wind." I watch even fruitful individuals go around like chickens with their heads cut off. To become progressively productive one should be "coordinating their blows so as not to strike the breeze." Be focussed and organize your undertakings. Work consistently and do what should be done first, at that point proceed onward to other, less earnest projects.

Maintain a strategic distance from the diversion. Life has numerous distractions. When they show up, they separate our concentration, and our vitality begins to move to "performing multiple tasks." Even though running a heap of clothing while at the same time working from a home office may be innocuous enough, exchanging unendingly from venture to extend is undoubtedly not. Attempt to kill your telephone or check messages just at endorsed times of the day. Individuals should regard that you are a bustling individual and comprehend when you don't hit them up inside 5 minutes. When they don't understand, you would prefer not to work with them in any case.

Evade obligation. Even though a few duties might be essential, by not connecting for things before you can bear the cost of them will assist you with avoiding the weight of conveying an additional obligation load. Have you at any point attempted to push a handcart that has been heaped up excessively high? Take a gander at your budgetary way with this point of view. Indeed, you may most likely push that heap gradually, yet begin losing air in your tire and you could before long end up ceased dead, or notwithstanding rolling in reverse.

Chapter 11: Introduction To Key Concepts

It is always wise to start learning something new by first cultivating an understanding of the fundamentals before moving on to something more complex. The human brain is a complicated entity; therefore, to understand how it works and how it influences your cognition, you need to understand some neuroscience, which is what we are going to do right now.

A Bit of Neuroscience

Neuroscience is the study of the human brain and the nervous system. Neuroscience works closely with several other disciplines including linguistics, mathematics, psychology, medicine, philosophy, computer science, chemistry, and engineering. Neuroscientists are scientists who study the evolutionary, behavioral, functional, molecular, cellular, medical, and computational aspects of your nervous system. Neuroscience is a relatively new branch of science that emerged distinctively in the 20th century, but that has grown rather rapidly since then.

From neuroscience, we know that the human brain weighs around 1.3kg and comprises of millions of neurons or nerve cells and millions of other cells referred to as 'glia' that connect to one another via a network of neuronal circuits and sub-circuits.

We also know that the human brain governs our thoughts, emotions, feelings, mood, as well as intelligence. It is also responsible for controlling our breathing, physical movement, sleep, and heart rate. Essentially, the brain is responsible for our survival and wellbeing; if it stops working, we stop living. Neuroscience focuses on the study of how the different neurons in your brain work and what causes the different changes within the brain.

While neuroscientists have discovered a lot about the human brain and figured out its connection with many ailments such as Alzheimer's disease, many things about the brain remain unexplored. Some things we still don't know about the human brain include how chronic pain develops and how to stop it effectively, how certain regions of your brain are more prone to disease compared to others, the true nature of human consciousness, and many other ambiguities and areas like these.

Let us now learn the relationship between learning and memory:

Relation between Memory and Learning

Because of the close association the two share with one another, Memory and learning are terms we often use interchangeably. While the two appear to mean the same thing, they in fact do not.

Memory is the ability to recall one's past experiences whereas learning is a process that modifies subsequent behavior. For instance, you learn French by studying and understanding it and then you speak it by retrieving from memory the words learned.

Your memory is the superior intellectual and logical cognitive process that describes the temporal aspect and dimension of your mental organization. Memory is essential for all types of learning because it allows us to encode information, store it, retain it, and finally recall the required information when you need it.

Memory is more of a record left behind after the learning process occurs. In this manner, memory is dependent on your learning, but learning things is also reliant on memory because you use the knowledge already stored in your memory to serve as the framework to build new linkages and associations. For instance, if you had used landmarks to memorize a certain route, you will employ the same technique the next time you have to learn a new route. Linkages like this help you learn new things easily based on the already formed associations saved in your memory. The more extensive your framework of existing knowledge, the easier it will be to build new linkages and learn things.

Your memory plays a fundamental role in your life. It saves your experiences and memories, and provides you with the possibility to reuse the past and present experiences to make decisions about the future. It also allows you to connect different patterns and make better, informed decisions based on the experiences you have had in life. Memory, in that regard, is a subjective, intelligent, and active reflection of your life experiences. It directly relates to your learning as the two co-exist, but you must not confuse the terms or use them to mean the same thing.

Let us now look at the different stages of memory and learning.

Stages of Memory

The three major processes involved in the memory creation process are:

Encoding

This refers to converting the information you receive into a specific form of data that your brain can save into your memory. This is the first step your memory puts in operation to learn something.

Storing

This refers to the stage that involves safely securing the encoded information in your memory. This happens when you successfully learn a piece of information or concept.

Retrieving

This refers to re-accessing the information encoded and stored earlier. When you need to recall some information, you retrieve it from your memory. To reinforce your learning or make use of that to make a decision or perform an action, you retrieve the learned piece of information from your memory.

Stages of Learning

Learning something has four main stages, but we do not necessarily cycle through all the four stages every time we wish to learn something.

Unconscious Incompetence

Unconscious incompetence happens when you are blissfully ignorant of something and are unaware of the knowledge or skill gap that exists. This stage is what we normally refer to when we use a phrase such as 'you don't know what you don't know.'

Conscious Incompetence

This stage occurs when you become conscious of a knowledge or skill gap and comprehend the significance of acquiring that knowledge or skill. This stage often signals the desire to start learning something. For instance, if you understand why you need to learn how to use Microsoft Excel to do well in your job, you opt for a course in that area.

Conscious Competence

The conscious competence stage occurs after you learn how to use the knowledge or skill you have acquired, but need to practice more and exercise hard work and conscious thought so that you can successfully perform a certain task.

Unconscious Competence

This stage occurs when you have enough experience with a certain skill to the extent that you can carry it out easily and even unconsciously on your own. When you successfully learn how to drive, you do not need to give yourself conscious instructions or remind yourself to apply the brakes when needed; your foot automatically moves to the brake pedal and presses it.

The different stages of learning and memory clearly show how the successful functioning of the two is inter-dependent. In the next chapter, we shall build on the knowledge you now have to cultivate a deeper understanding of how the human brain actually works.

Chapter 12: Four Types Of Learning And How To Learn Most Effectively

Have you ever wondered how you could use your senses in learning so that learning is easier? Because learning can become a lot easier if you know your strengths and weaknesses.

Every type of learner - whether child or adult - has his way of learning the most natural way. Depending on the kind of learning, we use different senses to understand better, understand and remember content.

In this chapter, we introduce four types of learning. Get to know your strengths and get ideas on how to use them while learning.

Which type of learner am I?

From experience, we know that there are different ways of learning. Some may well remember a reading material when they read it, others when listening to a speaker and others who learn more easily when they are writing or sharing their contents with fellow learners.

When children learn faster or slower in school, this often has nothing to do with the intelligence of the children, but with different types of learners.

We use our sense organs to learn. In addition to eyes and ears, this also includes the sense of smell, taste, and muscle. The learning material reaches our memory through the sensory organs involved. Since the individual sensory organs are different in each person, this means that there are different types of learning.

Based on the sense organs involved in learning, we, therefore, speak of auditory, visual, communicative and motor learning types.

Find out which type of learner you are. Then you can capture and anchor information in the way that best suits you. You do our free test: Which type of learner am I?

The learning type of determination is about tendencies. Effective learning requires the most significant possible participation and use of all senses. For example, if you are audibly weak, you should be careful not to take information by ear. Because you will then keep little of the information, complement your information intake with other learning methods that are more yours.

It is helpful if you memorize and process the learning material via as many sensory channels as possible. Because the more fields of perception in the brain are involved, the more mental connections can be made to the subject matter. In turn, you can increase your attention and motivation to learn and achieve higher learning success.

Learning types are usually mixed types. Some people learn well under time pressure and people who learn better on their initiative. Some like a slight noise and others need absolute library silence. Similarly, many blended learning types best learn in a combination of different situations and environment variables.

There are probably as many types of learners as there are learners.

An important part of self-knowledge is to know how to learn the most straightforward way or what learning to learn. The most reliable way to find out your learning method is to observe yourself and remember how you have achieved the most significant learning success so far.

If you want to improve the learning outcomes of children, then find out which type of learning the child prefers. Take a learning content that the child finds difficult to understand and paint a picture (visually), read the material (auditory), talk to it about it and let it explain (communicatively) or do an experiment, use gestures, go in the room up and down (motor). In which learning method did the child understand the substance most quickly / easily? Complete all further learning content with the corresponding learning methods.

The four learning types: 1. Learning by listening - The auditory learning type

The auditory learner can easily record, retain and reproduce the information it has listened to. He can follow oral explanations and process them. For him, explanations sound coherent; he can figure it out, they sound right.

To understand the physical law "pressure equal to force through the surface," the auditory learning type has an explanation of this form. "If one exerts a particular force vertically downwards on an object, it becomes due to the relatively large contact area of the object - the pressure on the plate on which the object is located has no significant effect, but if we reduce the area of contact of the object with a constant force, the pressure will pierce the plate. "

The auditory learner learns best when listening to the learning material (e.g., via audio CDs) by reading the text aloud or listening to another. He can memorize very well by speaking the text aloud and having verbal responsibilities.

Auditory learners often have self-talk while learning. Tell the learning content aloud, tell others about it, invent a song and sing it to yourself. Auditory learners feel quickly disturbed by ambient noise and usually do not like music in the background.

Learning aids: audio CDs, talks, lectures, music, quiet environment (no background noise)

2. Learning by seeing - the visual learning type

The visual learner learns best by reading information and observing the course of action. It is easier for him to memorize content when he visualizes it in the form of graphics or images. He finds explanations plausible, he has the insight, if he has understood something, if not, and he has to take a closer look at the material.

To quickly understand the physical law, "pressure equal to force through the surface."

The visual learner likes to read, look at pictures, illustrations or graphics to understand the facts. He needs a pleasant learning environment and enjoys working with panel paintings and written documents. He writes and takes information by seeing and showing. He particularly remembers what he has read and understood. Paint mind maps, pictures, work with colored pencils or markers. Use flipcharts or paper walls, work with video films or television reports on the topic. Imagine pictures as learning content when presented to you.

This type of learning can easily be distracted by the visual disorder.

Learning aids: books, sketches, pictures, learning posters, videos, learning cards.

3. Learning through conversation - the communicative learning type

The communicative learning type learns best through discussions and discussions. For him, the linguistic examination of the subject matter and understanding in the dialogue is of great importance. He has to talk through explanations - discuss them with others. Helpful in conversations is to be able to take both the position of the questioner and the explanator.

The communicative learner has to have a topic explained by a classmate (or colleague) and discuss it extensively to understand and keep it. The physical law "pressure equal to force through the surface" he understands best in conversation with others.

The communicative learner needs exchange and entertainment for learning. Discuss all information, disagree, encourage others to think and talk about topics, ask questions. Join group discussions, play role-playing games with fellow learners. Tell others what you have learned and ask questions.

Learning aids: dialogues, discussions, study groups, question, and answer games

4. Learning through movement - the motor learning type

The motor learning type determines best by performing actions themselves and in this way, understands. It is important for him to be directly involved in the learning process and to gain independent experience through "learning by doing." He understands explanations; they feel right. He explores topics and develops them.

This type of learning is easiest to learn when doing something, such as trying things out, role-playing and group activities. Build things, compute or refuel computational tasks with the material, run distances, and measure distances. Motor learning types are an excellent reminder of the information that they have received through movement, action, and feeling.

The physical law "pressure equal to force through the surface" understands this learning type the fastest if he experiments. The motor learning type has to be able to understand this fact in one's own body.

Move around while learning - walk up and down the room, repeating the material and complementing it with gestures and facial expressions. Find suitable objects for the learning material that you can touch. Do experiments whenever possible.

Learning aids: (rhythmic) movements, copying, group activities, role-playing games.

Criticism And Application Of Learning Types

Nobody learns with just "one sense." Humans are sensual beings and always experience the world above all senses. Therefore, it would be inappropriate in teaching practice to divide a class into different "types of learning" and to teach accordingly. Particular learning areas such as "tying shoes" can only make a visual type by "doing it yourself," i.e., by learning to learn motor skills. The mentioned learning types are only a valid perspective. Many other factors - such as motivation, interests, and the learner's personality - also play an important role.

Regardless of which learning method you prefer, try to include as many senses as possible in your learning process. Because: The more different we acquire our learning material, the more diverse the possibilities of remembering and retaining. Therefore, the reminder rate increases significantly, the more senses are involved in the learning process:

Listen only 20%

Only seeing 30%

Seeing and hearing 50%

See, hear and discuss 70%

Seeing, hearing, discussing and doing it yourself 90%

This concludes my little work. I hope I have made you curious, ask yourself what type of learning you are.

Chapter 13: The 'How' Of Nlp

Let us understand how NLP works, before we learn the ways to implement it. "Modalities" is the concept on which NLP is based upon. Modalities are the simplest form of each experience that we have in our lives. Representation of various physical and emotional senses like, visual, auditory, olfactory and gustatory senses are what modalities consist of.

Depending upon the experience, modalities are further divided into sub-modalities. For example, the sub-modalities for visual modality will be brightness, colour, clarity etc. These sub-modalities coming together make a unique experience pertaining to a particular sense.

To achieve a desired experience, NLP works by adjusting the knobs on each sub-modality. By adjusting the level of sub-modalities, an existing experience, assumed as fixed in nature, can be altered and perceived differently by the brain. The replacing of the altered experience with the original one in our unconscious mind brings about a modification in our actions.

This has an analogy to the working of music equalizer in our music system. When the knobs on each frequency level are altered, a different genre of music is produced even though the song is same. With the changed levels of sub-modalities, a present incident might not appear that bad, than it did in the past. Now, let's see the steps to incorporate the NLP system in our lives

First, analysis of your behavior pattern is important. Your actions should be known well beforehand, as NLP works on modifying our actions. Taking note of how you behave and react in a particular situation is important. It's better to carry a record with you and jot down your actions in it as taking mental notes can be exhausting and confusing after a point. Every action should be note down in detail, along with the circumstances that triggered it. Eventually, you'll find the way your mind has set itself, a pattern in your actions. The sub-modalities should also be note down so that you can adjust their levels later. This will make your mind more susceptible to changes, freeing it out of this rigid structure.

Here, you need a comparison tool with respect to which you can modify your actions. For this step, note down the activities of other people in the same situations as yours and then observe the two sets of people. One doing better and one doing worse than you in the field of concern will help you in making a different column for both the sets. Thus, helping you in comparing your activities and also to analyze them in your comparison table.

After your observation and comparison, deduce the information to implement it in your life. As NLP is a goal oriented program, set your goals before you proceed with this step. If a concrete goal isn't set while implementing it, you'll tend to get more confused and there will be no results. There are also chances of backfire if there is unnecessary data clutter in your mind. So, make sure you have a goal and work accordingly towards it.

Next up is formulating a plan that's best suited to your goals. Formulate the plan by making use of the behavior pattern you noted down. To achieve the same goal two people might have two different plans as each person behaves in a different way. This individuality is a key component of NLP. Find out the positive and negative traits in your behavior by comparing your actions to the reference subject's actions. Keeping track of the modification you're trying to make and the level of success in it, modify your conduct accordingly. Notice the changes that have occurred by comparing your current level of sub-modalities with your original levels.

Once NLP is launched, track your progress frequently. While implementing the program, noting down every progress and failure is important as this will help you in rediscovering your weakness and strength. Don't be disheartened easily, as it's difficult to achieve success in the first try itself. Carry your confidence by perfecting your imperfections and applauding yourself for every successful step that you have taken.

The final step is to keep the plan flexible. When you are near your goal, you might feel a need to include new steps in your arrangement. But sometimes, some modifications are not required, as they don't influence your performance as such. They will consume your energy and still not give you any results. So, it's better to discard these steps. Make sure not to be too hasty near the end as this knowledge is attained only when you follow the plan properly since the beginning. In case you wish to modify your goals near the end, make sure you don't incorporate a lot of changes. Make a new program altogether if a lot of changes are required or else, as a consequence, you will stray away from your original target.

Chapter 14: Learn Any Skill Quickly & Easily

You and your colleague are both web designers working for an advertising company. You both took up the same bachelor's degree but you made it to the top 5% of the class while he barely even passed it. The two of you eye the same promotion - he brought home the bacon.

What could have gone wrong?

The times are changing and what excessive attention people used to put into formal education are now rapidly replaced by evolving skillsets that give companies and businesses a competitive advantage in the professional world. And no one is to blame.

With the world becoming more fast-paced, achieving expertise in one domain may not be enough to sustain - let alone advance - your career. We are looking into an era of multiple intelligence now and the more you know, the greater chances you have to succeed.

However, acquiring new skills is not the simplest thing to do. When done traditionally, it would take years for you to master a new one. Research would tell you that learning a new skill will require around 10,000 hours of your time. Mind you, those are a lot of hours. If you do the math, that would take around 416 days - no sleep, no breaks.

Now, who has that kind of time?

The 10,000-hour Myth

To continuously practice one skill in a span of 10,000 hours requires a great deal of dedication and discipline. But if this really is an inflexible fact, how do you explain someone who gets ridiculously good at a new language, skateboarding, or painting in a week's time? I'm pretty sure you must've encountered a similar experience at some point in your life but unfortunately, it's hardly a rare occasion and doesn't make you anymore of a genius.

The fact of the matter is that there is more to this 10,000-hour rule than what mediocre information sources explain.

These crazy long hours are findings of researchers that studied top performers of complex and advanced skills as in the case of track and field and chess. It's a given for athletic and logic skills to require more time to practice. More so, if you're planning to join the all-stars.

If your goal is not the A-league and the purpose of your training is simply to get better and not the best, then learning a new skill may not be as intimidating as you think it would be. And it most definitely won't take you 10,000 hours.

The findings of Kaufman's research tell us that it is possible to learn a new skill in a feasible amount of time - 20 hours to be exact. So how does one go from a whopping 10,000 hours to a doable 20 hours?

On the other hand, author and skill-trainer Tim Ferriss said that it would only take 6 to 12 months before one can master a new skill at expert level or what he would regard as the top 5% of the practicing population. Language, he especially stressed, can be learned and functionally used in 8 to 12 weeks' time!

Both personalities suggest that acquiring new skills is actually quite simple but one would need the right techniques and motivation to get started.

What Hinders People from Learning a New Skill?

There are times we find ourselves having extreme difficulty to initiate the process of learning a new skill. We usually attribute it to external and internal factors such as lack of time, capacity, intellectual ability, and whatnot. In reality, we really do have what it takes to learn something - we just hesitate to commit.

Here are some of the factors that hinder us from learning a new skill:

Fear of Failure

You don't start something because you fear unsuccessful outcomes. It could be that you're not very comfortable dealing with unfavorable situations so not engaging in the activity at all would be the safest choice to protect your pride and self-image.

Say, you are to take a language proficiency exam. Instead of investing your time trying to advance your knowledge on a specific language, you put off all the work and comfort yourself by thinking that it's okay to fail because you never tried to pass anyway.

Feelings of Frustration

Learning a new skill requires a lot of patience and effort. One would usually undergo a series of trial and error procedures before fully mastering a specific skill. This, of course, is all part of the process but is not one to be favored by the faint-hearted.

Imagine yourself learning the basic task of baking shortbread cookies. Your first try came out burnt, the second one came out too salty, and another came out looking like a work of Picasso. After several attempts, you still keep failing. By this time, all that pent-up energy from failing makes you want to throw a fit and quit everything. Again, the goal is to overcome this urge and rise up against your worst adversary - yourself.

Too Many Distractions

There are just so many things we could do besides learning a new skill. However, those "many things" aren't always as productive. We fail to kick off learning at a good start because we have other matters that divide our attention. As the famous saying goes, "You cannot serve two masters at the same time." That means you cannot learn a language and watch your favorite Netflix show concurrently or master how to use Photoshop while playing a game of Assassin's Creed online.

These activities, however entertaining they may be, can take years of your life without you even noticing it. In general, they serve a good purpose such as being an effective outlet for built-up stress. However, anything done in excess can impact your life negatively and in this case, dull your interest to learn something new and give you more reasons to procrastinate.

The Illusion of Not Having Enough Time

This factor coincides with the preceding ones in which we program ourselves into thinking that we can definitely learn a new skill if only we had the time. Let me tell you something – you are never going to have enough time unless you change that train of thought.

Saying "I'll learn the basics of Japanese when I get some free time" or "I can't start learning how to cook because I only have so little time off work" are illusions you create for yourself to maybe avoid (1) failure, (2) frustration, or make more time for (3) other distracting activities.

These negative factors will always try to weigh us down and keep us from doing something more productive. So the challenge always lies in how we rise above these influences in order to continually grow our potentialities as a person and professional. And the sooner you find that motivation, the faster you'll be able to apply the techniques and methodologies necessary to help you learn skills faster.

How to Gain and Maintain Confidence Necessary for Learning a New Skill

In the case of skill-learning, repelling a negative force will require the help of a positive one. So the best way to gain the motivation needed to learn a new skill is to counter all fears, doubts, and excuses with positive reinforcement. And here are the big pluses we need in order to keep ourselves driven:

Simple and Feasible

Before we start any task, it is important that we gauge its difficulty level and compare it to what facilities we have – to make sure that everything needed to learn a new skill is realistic and readily available. It is also advised that we look into skills we already have and see if these can be used to acquire a new set of skills. Making a personal inventory of what you can do and what you'd like to learn can help you create a good start.

Complex skills will require more of your time and efforts. Also, they are more likely to bring you frustration after a number of failed attempts. If you are just beginning your skill acquisition journey, it would be best to start with something simple.

Because, more often than not, simple skills have higher probabilities for success. And succeeding in your first sessions of skill training will surely boost your confidence to continue learning a particular skill.

Early Outcomes

For each new skill you learn, there is a corresponding time estimate of how long it'd take you to master it. When the difficulty level is up, so does the time you'll need to train. But it is necessary to know that not all complex skills equal higher utility. Sometimes, simpler skills prove to be much helpful in practical applications. You just need to know which ones reap the most results with the least amount of time and materials.

Cooking, for example, is a complex skill that can be simplified into a more doable version. In the book, The 4-Hour Chef written by Tim Ferriss, he let us in on a little secret that can make me, you, and everybody else in the world for that matter, cook like a world-class chef. Not only does the book apply to cooking, it generally unlocks everything you'll need to master most skills known to man.

Sense of Accomplishment

After completing each training session successfully and realizing that your new skill is displaying identifiable results (being able to converse with a Chinese native after practicing Mandarin in a span of 10 weeks, for example) can give you an overwhelming feeling of accomplishment plus a great boost in confidence.

Knowing that you have the capacity to learn something and having concrete proof of your development allows you to trust yourself better. This newfound confidence plays a great role in motivating you to further your training and advance your skill levels – erasing most of your previous doubts and fears about learning something new.

Learning Skills Fast

It's Sunday. In your household, Sunday means laundry day. You have 6 people living under one roof and you're on duty. You have a mountain of assorted clothing each having a different color and you know that some colors don't jive well with others – especially the tidy-whites. There's too much that it seems impossible to start or finish. After a few sighs and urging whatever willpower you have left, you started sorting out the items by color and kind. Two or three hours later, the laundry room was spick and span. You wondered how on earth you managed to finish everything in such a short amount of time. But hey, all's well that ends well.

What we have above is a metaphorical example of a method called deconstructing. It is the process of breaking down a specific skill into tiny, little sub-skills. Or as in the case of our laundry day example, it's when the big pile of clothing got sorted out into similar groups. You see, every skill has two or more sub-skills that can be identified through a process called "clustering" – or putting together things that are alike. In the given scenario, the job got done faster after the clothes got sorted out. Well, same goes for learning a new skill.

When we chop down a pretty intimidating skill into realistically attainable sub-skills, we can hasten the process of skill acquisition. Think of it this way:

Before you learn how to bake, you first need to know how to whisk, sift, mix, and prep. You can't get out of bed one morning and simply decide you want to bake some muffins. First, you need to learn how to make the muffin batter before you start talking about baking them. Therefore we can say that mastering the sub-skills first is the fastest route to completing a new skill.

Another important method is Selection.

Keeping your attention span in-check for long hours is hard enough as it is – more so if you're to exhaust it for several months. Can you imagine memorizing vocab upon waking up and before going to bed every day? True enough, the thought alone can make you cringe.

Good thing we have alternative strategies.

Do you know that by changing the methodology you can change the rate of output as well? That's right, you can make learning new skills faster by changing the way you go about your training. As in the case of learning a new language, it would take you forever to memorize tens of thousands of vocabulary – and those are just words. Phrasing them, changing the tenses, constructing your own sentences are all tough areas you need to work on as well.

But, how about we trim tens of thousands to only 2,000?

You must be thinking that it's impossible for one language to only consist of 2,000 words. Well, it is impossible. But no one ever said you needed to learn each and every word in the dictionary before you can start a meaningful conversation using the language. This leads us to the process known as selection.

Instead of memorizing random words each day, how about studying a few general terms and phrases you'll most likely need to communicate. You'd be surprised to know that it only takes 4 verbal phrases, multiplied by a number of tenses, to hold a long, meaningful conversation in another language. All that's left is to feed your word bank with common terms that are essential for everyday use and communicating becomes a simple act of fill-in-the-blanks.

Learning How to Make Skills Last

Just when you've figured out the most difficult part – that is, learning a new skill fast – you wind up with another problem – how you can make them last. No one wants to put their effort into waste, especially after going through a lot of trouble to achieve something.

Skills are somewhat like relationships. They get dull when you fail to keep in touch. The world is changing as we speak and skills continue to evolve as we try to meet new demands. This means that if we fail to upgrade our skills diligently, time will come that our newly acquired skills will become obsolete.To keep the passion lit and fire burning, simply remember the two P's:

Practice

Probably the oldest one from the book but still a classic. Constant practice is essential to maintain the quality and accuracy of a skill. It keeps you from falling out of the trade and updates you with current trends. But practice requires a lot of self-discipline and commitment which makes it harder for people to follow-through after years have gone by.

Personal Merit/Demerits

Throughout our lives, we get to learn and master several skills – the number gets doubled when we actually make it our life's mission to learn more. This makes the maintenance part all the more difficult. Practice requires commitment but when you have so many, keeping everything not only becomes a challenge – it becomes an impossibility.

So the best way to keep them is to add value to them. Just like how we hold on to objects when they have sentimental or monetary value, skills are also easier to maintain when they provide us merit or help us avoid a demerit. After all, it's easier to train when something's at stake, right?

As a review, let us recall what we have learned in this chapter:

Learning more skills gives you competitive advantage inside and outside the workplace.

Skills can be learned faster using the right techniques and methodologies.

The common hindrances to skill development are fear of failure, feelings of frustration, distractions, and the illusion of not having enough time.

We can avoid these negative forces by countering them with positive skill-learning experiences.

Breaking down a skill into its sub-skills and learning it through a bottoms-up approach hastens the process of skill acquisition. (Deconstructing)

In skill training, you don't have to learn everything. You just have to focus on what's important. (Selection)

Constant practice as well as placing a specific value on the skill can help you maintain and improve it for a long period of time.

Chapter 15: Use Mind Maps

Mind Mapping is where students utilize a graphical arrangement to record thoughts and data about a specific point. They don't need to worry about placing things into a specific succession or utilizing a straight configuration. Mind Mapping programming gives the way to them to do this through their gadgets. Afterward, they can get to the mindmaps they have made, redesign them, transform them into customary notes, or basically use them as a source of perspective.

Mind Mapping has utilized in numerous orders. Advertisers, budgetary organizers, and numerous others use mind mapping

7.1 What is a mind map?

A mind map is a simple method to conceptualize considerations naturally without stressing over requests and structure. It enables you to outwardly structure your plans to help with examination and review.

A mind map is an outline for speaking to errands, words, ideas, or things connected to and orchestrated around a focal idea or subject utilizing a nondirect graphical design that enables the client to construct a natural system around a focal idea. A mind guide can transform an extensive rundown of dull data into a beautiful, vital and profoundly sorted out the outline that works in accordance with your cerebrum's common method for getting things done. A mind guide can be utilized as an improved substance to the board framework. It enables you to store every one of your information in a unified area to remain composed. With the different personality mapping programming programs out today, you can append documents to various branches for considerably greater adaptability. You can likewise change to different various perspectives so as to discover one that suits you best.

7.2 How to utilize mind maps

Mind maps can be more viable than other

conceptualizing and straight notetaking techniques for various reasons:

☐ It's a graphical device that can fuse words, pictures, numbers, and shading, so it tends to be progressively significant and charming to make an audit. The blend of words and pictures is multiple times preferred for recalling data over words alone.

☐ Mid maps connection and gathering ideas together through regular affiliations. This creates more thoughts, find further significance in your subject, and furthermore brief you to fill in more or find what you're absent.

☐A mind guide can without a moment's delay give you a review of an enormous subject while additionally holding a lot of data.

☐ It's likewise an instinctive method to sort out your considerations since mind maps copy the manner in which our cerebrums think—bobbing thoughts off of one another, as opposed to speculation straightly.

☐You can produce thoughts rapidly with this system and are urged to investigate distinctive inventive pathways.

7.3 Rules of Mind Mapping

Rule no. 1 expresses that you should begin at the focal point of a clear sheet of scene arranged paper. This appears to be progressively instinctive and helpful, so I wonder why you should damage this. This is a smart thought, if not a standard. Rule no. 2 encourages us to utilize an image for the focal thought of our mind maps. Here's a standard numerous individuals are not very wild about. While it may make mind mapping additionally intriguing, and the mind maps increasingly appealing, numerous perceive it isn't constantly conceivable—for instance, utilizing an image for unique topics is extreme for some. There is likewise the deep-rooted reason "I can't draw"

Rule no. 3 discussions about utilizing hues all through the mind map. There is consistently the risk of a rainbow gone unusual look with paying attention to this standard as well. I'd simply state—think about your motivation—is it a notetaking personality map, or a mind map intended to show others something? You should mitigate the neon green if it's to be introduced at a scholastic meeting (except if it's a mind mapping gathering).

Rule no. 4 encourages mind mappers to interface the fundamental branches to the focal picture and branch out from that. Sound counsel and this is by all accounts one of the focal distinctive highlights of a mind map. In case you're going to consider your creation a mind map, you must pursue this one.

Rule no. 5 essentially says, "Make your branches bent, natural and streaming, decreasing outward." Why will my mind maps be better on the off chance that you pursued this one? It's just on the grounds that this structure tenderly leads the eye to the branches from the focal thought and different branches. This is significant—recall those hallucinogenic hues? It additionally recognizes your mind maps from flowcharts, particularly with mind mapping programming.

Rule no. 6 is a fervently discussed one. It says, "Utilize one catchphrase for each line." Following this is getting increasingly troublesome, as mind mapping quits fooling around about its new symbol as a piece of visual information the board and portrayal framework. (Did I really compose that expression?). Here isn't the time and spot to discuss the advantages of doing this, get the job done to say that when doing hand-drawn maps for taking notes it is VITAL to focus on a single word per line.

Rule no. 7 requests that mind mappers use pictures all through their mind maps. This is incredible guidance, yet not for all. In the event that you must record highlights at an extraordinary speed, don't take a stab at drawing pictures and anticipate that they should be gems – stick figures will do the trick. In the event that you can, take a stab at including pictures later.

Rule no. 8 is the one I like best: Develop your very own style of mind maps. Mind maps are, at last, about you. On the off chance that rundowns work best for you, go for one with records. On the off chance that you can just work with green and red (every one of us has his/her peculiarities), proceed. Making your own style utilizing mind mapping programming might be a test—however not feasible.

Rule no. 9 states Use accentuation and show a relationship in your mind map. Good thought—accentuation recommends a chain of importance in ideas, which is frequently of significance. Once in a while, as we probably are aware so well, is everything equivalent throughout everyday life!

Rule no 10 the last one, says, "Use 'brilliant' progressive system, numerical request or layouts to grasp your branches." Embracing the branches isn't simply something tree huggers do, evidently! Suppose your mind map has two branches that are in one way or another related. Sectioning them together by either concealing them an alternate shading or by walling them in a blueprint, is an incredible method to show the connection between the two. Plainly, a useful rule.

7.4 Mind Maps vs Text Notes

1. Meeting Notes

An incredible method to take notes during gatherings is by utilizing a mind map. Infrequently do gatherings carefully pursue a motivation – there are consistently thoughts, criticism and innumerable considerations being talked about that should be caught. This is exceptionally hard to do with content notes in light of the fact that the inborn idea of content notes is to be direct. Notwithstanding, gatherings are infrequently direct and that is the reason mind maps are an extraordinary method to take notes during gatherings.

2. Book Summaries

We have shared a significant number of our book rundowns here and they have all begun as mind maps. Each great true to life book consistently has a lot of center thoughts and ideas and it is dependent upon the peruser to catch those. In the event that you have taken a stab at accepting notes as you read, I'm certain you have encountered how regularly you need to add more notes to another idea on another bit of paper, or you have to reference more seasoned notes utilizing bolts which can prompt exceptionally untidy notes.

Mind maps are perfect for outlining data, for example, that found in books. With branches as your principal ideas, you can tissue out ideas and thoughts with your (dissipated) notes and structure them for simple appreciation. On the off chance that you need to see a few instances of this, we parted with a portion of the mind maps that we used to compose posts.

3. Venture Management

There are huge amounts of programming applications and devices accessible for overseeing ventures, yet for littler tasks, mind maps are an incredible method to regulate and deal with an undertaking. A simple method to begin is to have your fundamental undertaking as the center thought and to have these branches set up:

Financial   limit
Assets
Individuals
Extension
Cutoff time

These are the essential segments of each venture and with a mind map, you can without much of a stretch do extend the executives. All you need is to arrange these branches and routinely audit them as you experience the task. You can anticipate more posts on this specific use, later on, however, don't be modest to give this a shot for yourself.

4. Considering

During my time at the college, mind maps were priceless – I would strictly utilize them in two different ways. The first was for taking notes during talks and contemplating. The subsequent route was to get ready for tests and tests by drawing an obvious conclusion. At the end of the day, I would have the mind guide of every one of my notes and afterward, I would attempt to interface all the principle ideas so as to comprehend the material at a crucial level. This enabled me to truly get a handle on the material without knowing the minor subtleties. When you comprehend the enormous strokes and ideas, usage (with a little practice obviously) of them and critical thinking will be a breeze.

5. Objective Setting

The objective setting has been around for a very long time and on the off chance that you have perused any book regarding the matter, you realize it's great practice to record your objectives. We are not here to differ with this as it's a demonstrated technique that has been maintained for a long time. In any case, we accept that the following level to recording objectives on pen and paper is by utilizing mind maps.
 Why?

Since it's visual. Your cerebrum can see the results – particularly in the event that you embellish your mind map with pictures. As we have composed on many occasions before here and in our pamphlets – having the option to imagine your objectives are massively significant and that is the reason mind maps superior to taking notes on paper. On the off chance that you're eager to begin utilizing mind maps for objective setting, at that point you unquestionably need to peruse how to set objectives like an Efficient Asian.

6. Critical thinking

There are numerous ways to deal with critical thinking however a well-known technique is the 5W + 1H diagram. This where you ask yourself a rundown of inquiries that you have to reply:

Who

What   Where

When

Why How

This is extraordinary to utilize mind maps for in light of the fact that as you extend each segment, you will, as a rule, see connections between your answers and that is something you can pinpoint at the forefront of your thoughts map. This will assist you in explaining the issue which makes the arrangement progressively clear as you experience all inquiries.

To begin, have your concern as your center thought in the mind outline have each branch speak to one of those inquiries. Attempt to respond to each address in separation when you start off and as you experience every one of them you will customarily go to an answer.

7. Conceptualizing

The way toward conceptualizing includes catching huge amounts of thoughts and a great deal of them in many cases have neither rhyme nor reason. Mapping the thoughts into a mind map enables you to effectively catch every one of the things that are put out and you can without much of a stretch later on structure the thoughts into something progressively important. We have expounded on the most proficient method to utilize mind maps for conceptualizing previously and we can strongly suggest you attempt this strategy. Whenever you have a meeting to generate new ideas, go the mind mapping course.

8. Information Management

Putting away notes on particular themes are basic with content notes. More often than not you simply end up with papers and dividers of content about a point that makes it hard to audit. Months or years down the line when you need to survey your notes, you will abhor yourself for not utilizing mind maps. On the off chance that there is anything specific, you need to audit it's extremely wasteful to attempt to find that somewhere close to several sections.

Rather, choose to utilize mind maps to deal with your insight bank. Particularly with programming based personality maps, it's totally astonishing how simple, basic and successful information the board can be. We will go more top to bottom on this in another post however one of the large preferences is that you can have records connected to your mind maps.

Suppose you need to make an information bank about business organizing. You have huge amounts of PDF records with tips, an Excel document with contact subtleties, a mind map on systems administration utilizing online life, and content notes of books, for example, Never Eat Alone and Love is The Killer App (both stunning books on business organizing). How might you make information manage an account with this data dispersed in various documents and in various arrangements?

The arrangement is to concentrate all the data and to have it tied in one spot. You can total this data into one personality map which will go about as your insight bank. In light of the utilization of connections maps, you can deal with this data in an organized way and in an arrangement that makes it simple to survey.

9. Completing Stuff

I will be the first to concede that a mind map isn't perfect as a plan for the day. Pen paper still rocks in that division. In any case, that doesn't imply that mind maps can't assist you with completing stuff. They totally can. Particularly in the event that you utilize a profitability technique, for example, Agile Results or you outline your GTD skylines in a mind guide and move the point by point undertakings onto your errand administrator. There are unlimited ways on how mind maps can assist you with completing things.

In the event that you need to see a down to earth case of this, look at our post on Agile Results and Mind Mapping.

10. Basic leadership

With regard to deciding, it's constantly a smart thought to have a rundown of alternatives to pick from. You can without much of a stretch do this with pen and paper, and with mind maps. Every technique enables you to delineate the alternatives however the enormous preferred position of mind maps is that you can make it visual for yourself. For a fact I can disclose to you that this improves things significantly when you attempt to weigh out various choices. Because of its visual nature, you can without much of stretch spot connections among choices and – particularly as you outline various situations it's simpler to make associations between alternatives so as to discover what the best choice is for you. Also, settling on choice trees (another successful method to assist you with settling on the correct choice) is substantially more powerful with mind maps.

Chapter 16: Change Your Mindset To Be Open To Learning

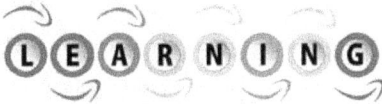

Learning is a life-long process, despite what the adage says about old dogs and new tricks. Children in school are constantly faced with new knowledge, which they absorb, and which then becomes integrated into their memories. So why is it that as adults, that type of learning seems to become more difficult?

It may be because children's young brains are still developing and forming neural pathways. Once humans reach adulthood, those neural pathways are set, and eventually they will begin to deteriorate. The mature human brain is already filled with memories and experiences. Learning new skills can feel daunting, because adult brains are seemingly 'out of room.'

The truth is, adult learning doesn't have to be difficult or seen as a chore. It is completely possible to reroute those neural pathways, create new ones, and develop constructive habits which will assist the learning process. Opening yourself up to new educational opportunities and adopting a positive attitude is are the first steps towards successful learning.

What Is the End Goal?

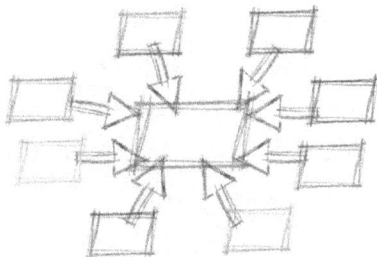

Before anyone can undertake any brain-training or academic study, it's important to determine the desired outcome. Do you want to have a better memory, or have you always wanted the ability to speedread? Are you looking to improve your study skills? Adult learners these days often find themselves in need of continuing education to further their careers, or make the decision to change career paths entirely and realize they are in need of training. It's important to identify the end goal of any educational undertaking **before** getting started.

What Is the Best Way to Learn?

Learning anything new requires the ability to receive and retain information. People learn in different ways, from childhood through adulthood, and that can change as a person ages. Someone who could learn quite well audibly (through retaining information they'd been told) as a youth may have grown into an adult who is a visual learner, needing to see or read the information for themselves. Still others are kinesthetic learners, meaning they retain knowledge through tactile, hands-on methods. While most people learn through a combination of styles, it will always be easier to acquire new knowledge if you know your preferred method of learning.

Exercise: Write down five random nouns, and on a separate piece of paper, draw simple pictures that represent five different random nouns. Study the list of words and the drawings for a short time, about 2-3 minutes apiece. Put the notes away, and wait for 24 hours. After a full day, try to first recall the five written words and then the five drawings. Did you remember more of the words or the drawings? Did you learn more by reading and writing, or by drawing and doing? To test your audible learning skills, have someone else read you a list of random words. Again, wait 24 hours and see how well you recall the list.

There **is** a caveat to learning styles, as some recent studies will suggest. While knowing what style of learning works best for you is a wonderful tool, you'll still have to be flexible in your learning and put in the hard work of studying. Some experts say that to truly learn, a variety of study material works best to stave away boredom. This isn't to say learning styles are invalid, it is to say that sometimes you may have to watch a film when you'd rather read, or put in the extra effort on a hands-on project when you'd rather not. It's all a part of opening yourself up to learning.

Ask, "Am I Personally Ready to Learn?"

Preparing to acquire any new skill or knowledge doesn't have to be nerve-wracking. By identifying your educational goal and your primary learning style, you've begun to set yourself up for success. Be open-minded and practical about your goals. Rome, as they say, wasn't built in a day, and a brain doesn't get rewired overnight. Studying and learning takes effort. Habits are built and broken over days and weeks, and sometimes even months and years.

Don't despair if you've never been the best student! In this book, you'll discover a myriad of techniques to benefit all kinds of learners. The most important thing is to be willing and eager. Maybe you've heard of some of the methods outlined here, and thought to yourself, "There's no way that will work for me!" But if you maintain an open mind and an enthusiastic attitude, there's nothing you can't learn and no strategy you can't employ.

Open Yourself Up to New Things

Do you remember as a child being told to try a new food? Maybe your mother even said, "Try it! You'll like it!" Sometimes you tried it and it was delicious, and sometimes you flat out refused. Fast forward twenty years, and you decide to try that same food as an adult. Turns out, that food is amazing! Isn't it a shame that you wasted two decades thinking you didn't like it?

The point is, you'll never know if you like anything until you've tried it, and you don't know just how much you can learn until you put your mind to it. Going into a task convinced that you'll fail will set you up for failure. Many of the learning techniques in this book are best practiced if you consider your brain to be a blank slate.

When you are open minded about learning, you can find yourself achieving things you may never have thought possible. Maintaining an open mind allows you to be more receptive of new concepts, gives you a better understanding of opposing or contrasting points of view, and helps you to be more confident in your ability to learn.

Being an open minded learner will also strengthen your critical thinking skills. While discovering a new learning technique is wonderful, being able to apply it beyond basic exercises is the key to making the technique a permanent part of your psyche. After all, if you can't apply the method in everyday life, what good is it to you, and what have you really learned?

The Building Blocks of Learning and Confidence

When small children learn to read, they don't go immediately from cardboard picture books to **War and Peace**. Becoming a confident reader takes plenty of time and practice, and it is a beautiful thing to watch a toddler sounding out their first words grow into an elementary-schooler who can read sentences and understand context. Adult learning functions in much the same way, but without a doting parent or a favorite teacher to mark milestones, there isn't nearly as much applauding and encouragement going on. Adult learners need to be their own cheerleaders to become more confident in their skills.

Breaking down learning tasks into small segments can be a great way to measure your achievements against your goals. If you are working on a skill in which you've never had any experience, make a list of the components of that skill and work on one component at a time until you can put them all together. The satisfaction of reaching those small milestones will keep up your learning momentum and motivate you to hit the next mark. Several of the following chapters will touch upon this skill, which is known as 'chunking'.

You should also confide in someone about your goals, like a partner or spouse, or your friends or family. You can ask them to provide you encouragement through the learning process. If you are working to improve your memory, tell them what techniques you're using and ask for assistance if necessary. Maybe you'd like help with flashcards or lists, or maybe you need to ask your partner to allow you a little quiet study time every day. No matter your goal, sharing it with your loved ones will hold you accountable and provide you with a support system. Hearing positive feedback and encouraging words will help you become more confident in your skills.

Consider the Practice of Mindfulness

We've all heard of the term 'mindfulness', but what does it really mean and how can you apply it to become a stronger, faster learner? Mindfulness is a state of awareness, of being in tune with your senses, and of being able to focus on the present moment and on a precise task. It's also about having the ability to self-regulate your actions and emotions to maintain an open mind and a sense of curiosity.

Have you ever felt like you did a sleepwalk through an everyday task? We've all driven somewhere on autopilot, or had a 'did I close the garage door?' moment. Chances are good that you did indeed close the garage door, because it's part of a routine so ingrained that you don't **have** to think about it. When we go about our business in the same way every day, we tend to lose awareness of what we're actually doing.

To actively practice mindfulness is to take the time to focus on each moment as it occurs. Instead of getting in your car and thinking about a hundred other things on the way to the office, think about the feel of the steering wheel in your hands. Look at the bright colors of the traffic lights, or count off how many stop signs you navigate through on your daily route. You'll be surprised to find how little you know about what's found in the distance between your home and workplace.

There are other ways to practice mindfulness, including mindful meditation. If you can incorporate just a few minutes of mindfulness into each day, you'll find yourself feeling calmer, more open-minded and clear-headed, and better able to focus on necessary tasks, including learning. The great thing about practicing mindfulness is that it doesn't cost anything, except for a little bit of your time. Here's how to get started:

Set aside the time- It's important to dedicate time if you want to practice mindfulness. It doesn't have to be very long, maybe 10 or 15 minutes every day. Once you've become experienced at mindful meditation, you can adjust the time you spend on it each day. You'll begin to know how much time you need.

Find a quiet place- If you want to be able to focus and clear your head, it's important to have a place where you can do so, where you can be uninterrupted and sit peacefully.

Be comfortable- Be sure that you're physically comfortable when you have your mindfulness sessions. Have a cozy place to sit, wear unrestrictive clothing, and make sure the temperature is adjusted properly. The idea is to reduce any physical distractions so that you can focus on the mental exercise of mindfulness.

Breathe easy- You want to calm your brain by focusing on your breathing. Feel each breath, and try to keep it even and steady.

Pay attention to your body- Think about how your body feels as you are sitting still. Can you feel your heart beating? Are your arms and legs comfortably at rest? Try to make yourself aware of how every inch of your body feels.

Don't wander away- Whenever you feel your thoughts starting to wander, bring yourself back to the point of focusing on your breath. Don't get mad at yourself for daydreaming- the purpose of mindfulness is not to completely empty your head. You just want to teach yourself to focus. You can go back to the steady breathing step and start over.

Be nice to yourself- It takes time to get the hang of mindfulness. Don't give up if you find your brain wandering more than you think it should be. The more you practice mindfulness, the better you will get at it.

Studies show that people who practice mindfulness have increased concentration and better memories. Those who practice mindfulness also have less stress and anxiety, sleep better, and have greater cognitive function. There also seems to be a link between mindfulness and slowing the progression of Alzheimer's disease. Students who practice mindfulness perform better on standardized tests and report a greater capacity to retain information.

Get Excited About Adult Learning

Of course, one of the best things about learning as an adult is that the subject matter can be anything you wish! There's no standard curriculum in the school of life, so if you want to teach yourself to speedread or learn to improve your memory, do it! If you want to learn logic puzzles or how to paint watercolors, do that, too! The possibilities are endless with adult learning, and this book will give you the skills to learn anything you want. You don't have to be like our poor friend Calvin- you aren't bound by the constraints of a first-grade syllabus.

The learning skills you'll find in these pages will help you better understand the complexities of memory and retention, and will aid you in any field you intend to study. Gaining new knowledge is human nature; it's what moved our species from the Stone Age through the Industrial Revolution to the technological era of today. It's one of the most wonderful things about humans...we will always be hungry for the next big advancement in learning and growth.

Chapter 17: Learning Techniques

Every student is different. Some students who are lucky enough to have photographic memories can retain everything they see even if they only see it once. Others learn efficiently only when they use visual aids.

Part of putting accelerated learning to work for you is learning which techniques mesh with your personal learning style. The more you understand your brain and how it learns, the better able you will be to single out the methods that are most likely to lead to success.

With that in mind, in this chapter I will describe several learning techniques that may help you fine-tune your learning process.

Sensory Reinforcement

You know that human beings have a total of five senses: sight, hearing, smell, touch, and taste. Most classroom settings, though, use one or two at most. In fact, the two most common are sight and hearing.

It is certainly possible to learn without engaging all five senses, but the more senses you involved in the process, the more likely it is that you will absorb new information and retain it for later use.

Let's look at a simple example. Imagine a student who is trying to learn about basketball. If all that student gets is a lecture about basketball, he will have an incomplete grasp of it at best.

Now imagine that the teacher shows the student a video of a basketball game. Now, he gets to see what he has learned in action. He may have a greater understanding of how the game works.

If the teacher hands the student a basketball, he can feel its weight and texture, smell the material used to make it, and even make an exploratory bounce or pass.

The student who has the opportunity to take the basketball outside, learn to dribble and pass, and take a few practice shots will have a far greater grasp of basketball than the one who merely listens to someone talk about it.

Each of these things shows the benefit of sensory reinforcement. When you learn something and get to see it in action, or have an opportunity to use it, then your brain works to integrate everything you have learned. Each part of the learning experience – auditory, visual, tactile, and physical – builds on the others.

Now, some subjects lend themselves to this sort of learning more easily than others. But here are a few examples of how you might be able to incorporate them:

☐ If you study a particular topic and aren't sure you understand it, try going to

YouTube and seeing if you can find an explainer video to help you along.

☐ Does what you read remind you of a song or a book or an experience? Think about why. Listen to the song. Seek out pictures to help you commit what you have learned to memory.

One area of learning where students openly embrace the idea of sensory reinforcement is in the study of foreign languages. Teachers in that field regularly show movies, teach students songs, and have them act out dialogues that include classroom vocabulary. They may even have students try traditional foods as part of their learning experience.

The benefit of this approach is that it engages all of your senses, providing your brain with a series of experiences to reference when remembering what you learned.

Active Recall

Human memory can be a fickle thing. The information you access most frequently is what you are most likely to remember when you search your mind for information.

For that reason, one learning technique that helps students excel is active recall, which emphasizes repeated recollection of information to strengthen the brain's ability to remember them.

One study had students pair up to study new vocabulary in a foreign language. In the study group, students were quizzed using flash cards and when they recalled a word correctly, it remained in their flash card rotation. In other words, each word was studied multiple times.

In the control group, students removed cards from the deck once they remembered them successfully. The results showed that the students who accessed the information they learned more frequently – the first group – remembered an average of 80% of the words they learned when quizzed later, while the control group remembered only 30% of the words they learned.

The takeaway here is that repetition is your friend. The more often you access a piece of information, the stronger the neural pathway to it becomes.

However just reading over your notes repeatedly is a very ineffective way to study any material. The key is to combine spaced repetition with the more active approaches described in this book.

Teach What You Learn

One of the best ways to accelerate your learning is to pass on what you know. When you take responsibility for somebody else's learning, you have

to break down information in a coherent way. The process of doing it ensures that you truly understand the topic.

Even if you don't have a willing student, you can use this technique by writing a mini lesson plan as if you needed to teach the subject. How would you approach it? What would you talk about first? Thinking about these questions can help you fill in gaps in your knowledge and understand a topic on a new level.

Use Mind-Mapping

Mind-mapping is a visual learning technique that can help you break down complex topics for later recall.

You can start by drawing an icon or symbol in the middle of a page to represent your main topic. Then, draw branches from it to include subtopics and related issues. For each thing on your mind map, draw a small picture. The process of conceptualizing pictures to represent ideas, and of linking topics to subtopics, helps you to put the information you learn into context.

Now that you have some learning techniques to consider, it's time to take the final step. In the next chapter, I'll tell you how to create a study plan that's built to help you overcome your obstacles to learning.

Chapter 18: Nutrition And The Learning Process

Suddenly, it's official. More brain power means you're smart. And smart is becoming HOT!

From poking fun at the nerds, we've come a long way to idolizing a superman who is, in his normal life, studious to the point of boredom. And people think he's sexy.

Do you suddenly see a pattern here?

People want to become smart - not only because it might win them more girlfriends and admirers. They understand that the corporate culture is slowly seeping into schools and colleges; the college drill is bleeding into corporate offices. What that means is you're expected to learn throughout your life, and learn it well and fast.

Of course, learning power plays an important part in your life – up to a point. After your first honorary degree and speaking assignment, every one takes it for granted that you're smart. They'll be quoting you and brushing shoulders with your eagerly. After all, who knows what Warren Buffet's IQ is? Who cares?

But this happens only after you've crossed the invisible limits of success and reached super-success. To get there, you need 100% of your brain power working for you – and then some.

While study techniques can make a substantial difference to your ability to learn and remember, there are certain other things you can do to ensure that your brain is giving you its all.

Food and brain power: Your brain is a part of your body. It is naturally affected by your diet as any other organ in your body. Eating right and eating well is the first secret to an efficient and healthy brain.

Some of the more common food supplements that can help your brain are:

• Gingko Biloba: The leaves of this plant increase the flow of blood to the brain and give the brain an instant boost. Used in the capsule form, it is also inexpensive and easy to find.

• Vinpocetine: This extract is taken from

the Periwinkle plant. It is used as a cerebral vasodilator which increases the flow of blood into the brain. This increases mental activity and alertness. Some studies show that this extract may be quite potent in enhancing memory.

• Phosphotidyl Serine: In scientific experiments, it has been shown that it can increase the rate of learning. It helps cell growth and prepares the cells for activity. It also stops memory decline. The best part is that this supplement has no known side effects.

• Saint John's Wort: There are no studies to show its effectiveness, but people swear by its calming effects. As discussed elsewhere, we are most open to learning when we are calm and confident.

Some food supplements may have unpredictable or undesirable side-effects. It is therefore advisable to consult with your doctor before you take them.

Do you like to eat? Being a junk-foodie will not help your brain. But indulging in the right kind of food can make you smart.

• Caffeine: Studies show that students

who have a foaming cuppa just before their exams actually do better. But there are indications that caffeine can affect your decision-making skills adversely. The effect of caffeine varies from individual to individual.

• Eat fish: Fish is brain friendly as it improves concentration and speeds up brain   waves.

• Go nuts: Eating nuts like hazel nuts and almonds may boost brain activity – at least in   the   short   term.

• Olive oil: This oil is high in mono-unsaturated fat. It improves memory. So splash it liberally on those greens and munch   away!

• Fiber: What goes into your body is almost as important as what goes out. Proper elimination is a prerequisite to good health. Holding in harmful and poisonous toxin can make you sluggish and slow. Fiber helps you flush out toxins easily.

• Vitamin supplements: Studies show that children score higher when they are on daily vitamin supplements.

• Become lean: High fat makes you slow. It assists the deposit of toxins in your body. Saturated fats can actually stunt the growth of brain cells. Overeating starves the brain because blood is redirected to the digestive process. Overeating produces fat globules which cut off the blood supply to the brain.
• Eat a good breakfast: A balanced breakfast is important to optimal mental activity. Since your brain needs carbohydrates and sugars to function well, a proper breakfast is a must. In one research children who ate breakfast had higher math scores than those who did not.
• Pile on the antioxidants: Antioxidants protect the cells of your brain. Some foods that are high in antioxidants are prunes, raisins, blueberry, garlic, kale, strawberries, spinach and raspberries. Red wine also contains antioxidants and seems to be good for the brain when used in moderation.

• Natural Vitamins: Vitamins like Vitamin C, Vitamin E, Selenium and basil are good for the brain. Some of the super foods for the brain include avocados, bananas, brewer's yeast, broccoli, brussel sprouts, cantaloupe, eggs, flaxseed oil, legumes, oatmeal, oranges, peanut butter, peas, potatoes, salmon, soy beans, tuna, turkey, wheat germ and yoghurt.

Keeping your body healthy is an important part of being smart. Here are certain things you can do to help your brain.

Shake a leg: The brain requires lots of fresh blood as oxygen is very important for its processes. Lack of fresh blood supply can cause concentration levels to dip. If you've been sitting in one place for too long, move about and bounce your legs for a minute or two. This gets your blood flowing and improves concentration as well as retention.

Reduce stress: Stress can cause brain damage. It also hampers the learning process because a stressed out mind is often unable to focus on the task of learning. Go bake some cookies or take a walk before you get back to your study table.

Stimulate yourself: Sing, play, laugh and feel good. This releases endorphines which lowers stress levels and enhances mental activity. Stimulating the brain through play, puzzles and other activities makes changes in the structure of the brain. Exercise you brain: Learn a new language, solve a crossword puzzle or start using your mouse with the other hand. Any activity that requires learning is exercise for the brain. Regular use of the brain generates new neuronal growth which augments your brain power.

Motivate yourself: If you believe that you are smarter than others, you will be. Techniques such as self-affirmation can help you. Celebrate your successes and think positive. Set goals. Have a game plan. Give yourself deadlines and stick to the dates.

Take a break: Taking a 5-10 minute break while learning helps you learn better. Sometimes a power nap can help you solve problems. When you get embroiled in something, change your focus and return to the problem after some time. Start meditating. It helps to calm your mind.

Chapter 6.0 Recap:

• Your brain is an organ that needs plenty of oxygen and lots of nourishment. Give it.

• Eating 'brain-foods' will make you smarter.

• A healthy brain lives in a healthy body. Get   physically   fit.

• Motivate   yourself.

• De-stress yourself. Take a break. Enjoy the   rain.   Start   meditating.

Chapter 19: Memory Mastery

"My brain power depends on my retained mastery of analyzing in detail of what's happening in my world my mind and body. I must continue to practice to retain my constructive and analytic powers. The goal is to be a master of my environment."
-Michael Merzenich

Easy Techniques You Should Know

Mnemonic devices are tools you can use to retain information more effortlessly. There are many different mnemonic types:

Music mnemonics - Songs and jingles are used mostly by children for example; to remember the 50 states in America. Children shouldn't be the only ones benefiting from this tool.

Note organization mnemonics - The method of note organization can be used as a memorization technique for example; when creating a food shopping list, you can categorize the items you need into the groups of items you'll get in order. If done correctly you won't have to even check your shopping list.

Visualizations mnemonics - Simply imagining a picture to create meaning to the word. This tool should not be overlooked for the power of envisioning will increase over time with a lot of practice.

Phrase mnemonics - For example; to remember the planets orbiting the sun - use My Very Educated Mother Just Served Us All Pizzas. (each first letter to represent the planet).

Chunking Mnemonics - break up information into smaller groups to make more sense. (organizing a basic set of numbers into format like a phone number) There is no limit to the ways you can use mnemonic devices as you practice this in your daily life you may be able to create your own mnemonic device or find ways to make them work uniquely for you.

Effectiveness of Mnemonic Link System

Another powerful memory system is the Mnemonic Link System. This is also called the chain method. To help you memorize a group or list of items, create associations between these items. For example, try to memorize dog, thirteen, window, yarn. These items look unrelated but you can make associations to help you remember. So, there is this dog who live in a house with the number 13 pasted on the window. This number dangles on a yarn. Another method is to make visual (with the mind's eye) associations. Create a mental image that a dog enters a house with a number 13 hanging by a yarn on the window.

Just as we covered in the previous chapter; Visualization and Association are the primary components used in most of the mnemonic devices. This simple system does have its limitations, for instance, there is no numerical order imposed when memorizing, hence, the practitioner cannot immediately determine the numerical position of an item; this can be easily solved by putting numerical markers at set points in the chain or by using the method of loci/memory palace.

Memory Palace or Method of **loci** (being Latin for "places")

The Importance that Ancient Greek and Roman Cultures Place on Memory.

This ancient Imagery mnemonic device was used by Ancient Greek and later Roman orators to memorize speeches. This method dates back to more than 2000 years ago when reading a speech from a script was frowned upon. The method of loci or memory palace was used to help their speeches that would last for hours.

Rhetoric is an art that aims to improve the capability of writers or speakers to inform and persuade. It makes sense that Greek rhetoric treatises would adopt the method of loci to have any advantage in giving persuasive speeches without skipping a step and forgetting an important piece. Imagine what this technique can do for our daily lives.

In this technique, the subject memorizes the layout of some building/home, or the arrangement of shops on a street, or any geographical entity which is composed of a number of discrete loci. When desiring to remember a set of items the subject 'walks' through these loci in their imagination and commits an item to each one by forming an image between the item and any feature.

A lot of memory contest champions claim to use this technique to recall faces, digits, and lists of words. These champions' successes have little to do with brain structure or intelligence, but more to do with their technique of using regions of their brain that have to do with spatial learning.

In cognitive psychology and neuroscience, **spatial memory** is the part of **memory** responsible for recording information about one's environment and its **spatial** orientation.

For example, a person's spatial memory is required in order to navigate around a mall.

Research has shown that the hippocampus which deals with visual-spatial awareness, is larger in London Taxi drivers than normal people. London 'cabbies' have to spend months, sometimes years, learning literally every street in the Capital before they are allowed a license.

The method of loci is a mnemonic device that uses a combination of tools our brains can relate with easier. Visualization and association which we have learned about before starting this chapter plays a large role in the method of loci. Spatial memory and story telling are great in combination for remembering because story telling has a beginning and an end in a chronological order that will help your mind envision the association and the information needed.

Those individuals who have trained them selves to use memory palaces effectively can rapidly recall things that would normally occupy one of the short-term memory slots. It's possible that they are hacking the part of the brain responsible for spatial awareness so when needed they can recall a map with numerical order of sequence.

Let's dig in for a Deeper Understanding
Build your very own personal mind palace.
Let's follow each step accordingly.

Put   in   the   Effort

Step one; you want to use a place that you are intimately familiar with. The best example is your home that has lots of details (furniture) and locations.

Step two; put the locations of your home or any place you are using into an order so that there is a set sequence as if you were walking through each different location. (from the front door to the last room in the house)

Number each living space or location.

Step three; create association hooks on the detailed (furniture) items that most stand out to you. To start off, you can make one or two hooks per room or if you feel ready, you may choose 5 hooks per room. Take note that the more hooks you have per room, the more information you'll be able to store in your mind palace like a file in a filing cabinet.

Next: Stand at the door way at each room and count off from left to right 1-5 hooks in the first room, then 6-10 in the next room, 11-15 and so on per living space.

Tip: Pick 5 big items that stand out to you so that you can easily imagine and recall.

For example; A stove, TV, Couch, computer, etc. Don't use the same item you used in one room in another. You may increase the number of hooks in your mind palace as you grow to remember larger and more abstract information.

Step four; Once you have numbered each hook from 1-20 or what ever number of hooks you have, now resit each hook from beginning to end 1-20 and resit it backwards from 20-1. Know it inside and out for you are in the process of creating an easy tool you can use to be great at memorizing anything. Don't be intimidated by this step, you already know these items in your house -were just putting the items in a number of sequence. If you have to write each one down and study it a little so that if someone asks " what is number 11"? -you are able to recall the hook item that is stored in the 11th slot, this is when you truly have created a strong memory palace.

After following step four; you now can use this method to remember anything from shopping lists, sequence of numbers to your to-do list and etc. We are using physical location to tie the information onto -so you now have an instant spatial association to create a strong image.

Putting your new skill to use

Starting off let's use our new skill to remember a basic shopping list.

Salad

Baby spinach

Blueberries

Oranges

Detergent

Paper towels

Window cleaner

You may think you can just remember this small list effortlessly but you can easily get distracted and miss one of these items. The plan is to make the shopping items more meaningful so that it's not going to be forgotten easily.

Conclusion

You have come to the end of this learning manual. I wish to thank you once again for downloading this book. I hope that it was able to help you understand why learning is so crucial to success and how to significantly boost your learning capacity. While learning is vital for doing anything successfully, knowing is just half the battle. The other half is action – the application of knowledge.

As such, I encourage you to immediately apply the tips and strategies you've learned in this book. By taking your sweet time, you run the risk of not taking any action at all and with that, end up back at square one. Remember that the brain can only retain so much without putting it into practice!

When I talk about action, I don't mean applying everything in one fell swoop. Take baby steps, reward yourself, and keep your eyes on the prize. When you've mastered one principle or lesson, start applying the next one, and the next one, and so on and so forth – until you've successfully become a master at education.

There is no border that separates the extraordinary from the average; it is simply the journey in which the individual chooses to take. Your passion is your shield and knowledge is your sword. Take on arms and fight your way to the very top. Know that your mind is truly unstoppable.

www.ingramcontent.com/pod-product-compliance
Lightning Source LLC
Chambersburg PA
CBHW060330030426
42336CB00011B/1273